THE
# CANADIAN
# INUIT DOG

# THE
# CANADIAN
# INUIT DOG

## ICON OF CANADA'S NORTH

# BY KIM HAN

**REVODANA**
PUBLISHING

REVODANA PUBLISHING

81 Lafayette Avenue, Sea Cliff, N.Y. 11579

ISBN: 978-1-943824-42-7

www.revodanapublishing.com

In loving memory of Siu-Ling.

For Bing, Jeff, Diane, Timothy, Kina, Yi Zhen and Jin.

# TABLE OF CONTENTS

# Foreword

By Allen Gordon

I met Siu-Ling Han in the early 1980s, when she was passing through my home community of Kuujjuaq, Nunavik. Little did I know that I would reconnect with her again in 2006, when I was seeking to get back to dog sledding with the original purebred Inuit Sled Dog.

Knowing that traditional Inuit Dogs were still in use in Iqaluit, Nunavut, I contacted Matty McNair, who put me in touch with Siu-Ling. She also had a fine team of authentic Inuit Dogs there, and her female was expecting a litter in a few weeks. I am grateful to her for my first two beautiful female *qimmiit*, sisters Tarqirk and Piqatik, the foundation of my dog team today.

*The Canadian Inuit Dog: Icon of the Canada's North* is a great book by Kim Han, written with passion in memory of her daughter and the tremendous love she has for her. Kim is ever so proud that Siu-Ling was able to enjoy life with the people of the north, even partaking in traditional sled-dog racing.

Kim writes about the toughest dog on earth, the only dog in the world that allowed humans for the first time to reach both north and south poles when attempts with different animals had failed. Kim also touches on a sad, dark history regarding the killings of sled dogs by the authorities. I was too young when it happened, but have heard many accounts and stories from elders. It brings to light the very wide communication gap that existed back then when governments arrived in the north. With a total lack of understanding of our culture, they merely saw the sled dog as a negative that needed to be controlled.

The aboriginal Inuit Sled Dog is not well known to this day. I still have to explain to visitors to my region of Nunavik that it is special, and a vital part of Inuit history across the Arctic. If it weren't for the Inuit Sled Dog, my Inuit ancestors would not have survived and travelled great distances to populate the Arctic.

Allen Gordon and his dog team in 2010. *Photo: Pierre Dunnigan. ©Makivik.*

Kim having written this book is very positive in delivering and spreading the knowledge about the Inuit Sled Dog, rather small in numbers, to a wide audience. — **Allen Gordon**

*Allen Gordon is a musher, tourism outfitter-guide and elected official in Kuujjuaq for more than 20 years. Executive director of the Nunavik Tourism Association and a fellow of the Royal Canadian Geographic Society, he founded the first Arctic Char fish hatchery in the eastern Arctic, and has been recognized by the Foundation de la faune du Quebec for his part in biodiversity efforts and the protection of wildlife habitats.*

# Preface

How I came to know and love
the Canadian Inuit Dog

W hy would a librarian from Ottawa, Ontario, who has never lived in the Arctic or managed a dog team write a book about the Canadian Inuit Dog?

My daughter, Siu-Ling, lived on Baffin Island, the largest island in Canada's Arctic Archipelago, where she owned a team of traditional Inuit Dogs. She started her dog team in 1999, after

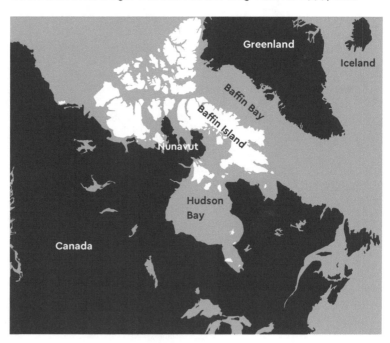

Canada's Arctic Archipelago.

acquiring Atsuli, Aiviq and Fiddich from her friends Lynn Peplinski and Paul Crowley, longtime Arctic residents and Inuit Dog owners. The only female on Siu-Ling's team was Lao, a gift from her friend Ken MacRury, an Inuit Dog authority and longtime Arctic resident. Ken taught Siu-Ling a lot about Inuit Dogs and dog sledding. He even helped her build a *qamutiik*, an Inuit-style sled.

Siu-Ling with Lao and puppies. *Photo: Elise Maltinski.*

When I visited Siu-Ling in Iqaluit, the capital of the northernmost Canadian territory of Nunavut, in 2001, she had two eight-week-old puppies, Toko and

Lao, the matron on Siu-Ling's team. *Photo: Siu-Ling Han.*

A *qamutiik*, an Inuit-style sled. *Photo: Siu-Ling Han.*

Rode (pronounced "RO-dee"), whom she had named after ski waxes. They were the offspring of Atsuli and Deneb, one of Matty McNair's females. Matty is a world-renowned polar guide and adventurer living in Iqaluit and a friend of Siu-Ling's. Matty and Siu-Ling bred and shared a number of Inuit Dogs.

When I saw Toko and Rode, it was love at first sight! They

Siu-Ling with Toko and Rode. *Photo: Debbie McAllister.*

were the cutest, chubbiest, cuddliest pups I had ever seen. Like two bouncy balls of fur, they darted here and there, happily sniffing and exploring everything in their paths when we took them for a walk in the tundra. That was the spark that ignited my interest in these captivating aboriginal dogs.

Lots of handling and regular socialization help an Inuit Dog learn how to take his place in the pack, and in Inuit society. *Photo: Lynn Peplinski.*

Siu-Ling loved her dogs and took special care to keep them healthy and happy by giving them individual attention, and bringing them up in a way that honored Inuit cultural tradition.

Then, out of the blue, life threw her a curve ball.

When cancer struck in the spring of 2003, Siu-Ling moved back to Ottawa for treatment, but went back to Iqaluit to be with her dogs after her treatment was completed. That year we decided to spend our family Christmas at Siu-Ling's in Iqaluit. Toko and Rode were two years old and had become full-fledged sled dogs. New additions had expanded the team even more.

During that holiday, Siu-Ling decided to take the family dog sledding. There are only five hours of daylight in Iqaluit in December, so we didn't have much time. With an average temperature of -9.4° F (-23° C), not to mention the wind chill, we had to be outfitted with Arctic gear and big, bulky boots that look like moonboots.

When we approached the dog yard, the dogs recognized Siu-Ling's pick-up truck right away and started howling and jumping up and down in excitement, enthusiastically wagging their big, bushy tails. It was as if they were saying: "Hello! We're here! Let's go for a run!"

Are we ready to go yet? *Photo: Thomas Godfrey.*

After greeting and petting each dog, Siu-Ling harnessed them and attached a trace to the harness, which has a *sanniruaq* (toggle ) made of bone or antler at the end. Each dog has its own trace, a long rope with a loop at one end that hooks onto the *sanniruaq*. It is easily unhooked to let the dog run loose without removing the harness. At the other end of the trace is an *uqsiq* (fastening ring) that connects all traces to the *pituk*, a

Near right: *Sanniruaq* (toggle) made of bone or antler. It is attached to the top of the harness. *Photo: Debbie McAllister.* Far right: *Uqsiq,* or fastening ring, which connects all traces to the *pituk* (see opposite page). *Photo: Madeleine Cole.*

looped rope that attaches the dogs to the *qamutiik*.

This was our first dog-sledding trip, and we were a bit apprehensive: There was nothing to hang onto, except for the backless seat of the *qamutiik*, which was lined with caribou fur. What if we fell off? How would we make the dogs stop? We couldn't possibly run after them in those big, bulky boots. Siu-Ling told us not

The orange rope is the *pituk*, which attaches all the dogs to the sled, or *qamutiik*. *Photo: Paul Crowley.*

to worry, and just sit and relax. That was easier said than done. When the dogs took off at her command, we almost fell over backward from the jolt, but managed to hang on to the *qamutiik* as we zipped up and down hills over the rocky, snow-covered tundra, the dogs pulling and panting, with tongues hanging out and tails waving like plumes.

In the autumn of 2005, Toko — who had proven himself to be a great leader — and Lao produced five puppies. After they were weaned, Siu-Ling brought them to Ottawa for the Christmas holidays. She had started to handle the pups since the day they were born, because it was important for them to get used to people and, especially, children. Our granddaughter and neighborhood children visited almost daily and took turns playing with the puppies during their stay in Ottawa. The

Two of the Toko-Lao puppies get some socialization from the author's granddaughter, Kina. *Photo: Jeff Han.*

pups were barricaded on my front porch, squeaking, squealing, fighting, biting, howling and yowling, climbing and tumbling over each other. Getting to know these dogs is to fall in love with them, and become fascinated by their astonishing attributes, which are described in this book. It is awe-inspiring to learn how much they contributed to humankind, and how little they asked for in return.

Siu-Ling continued to live life to the fullest and enjoy her time in the serene Arctic with her beloved dogs. They were one of

Connie Maley, Siu-Ling and Matty McNair take a well-deserved break on the Baffin Island trip. *Photo: Debbie McAllister.*

the reasons that made her life worth living, and in 2007 as well as 2008 she participated in the Qimualaniq Quest, a 200-mile (320-kilometer) race from Iqaluit to Kimmirut and back, placing third in 2007, and second in 2008. To celebrate five cancer-free years, Siu-Ling and her friend Debbie McAllister, a physician from Calgary, made plans for an ambitious dog-sledding and skiing expedition along the stunning eastern seaboard of Baffin Island with a tour through Sam Ford Fjord, starting in Qikiqtarjuaq, a hamlet on Broughton Island located along the east coast of Baffin Island, just north of the Arctic Circle, with Pond Inlet as their destination. Pond Inlet, or Mittimatalik in Inuktitut, is a picturesque hamlet on the northern tip of Baffin Island, near one of the eastern entrances to the Northwest Passage.

Siu-Ling and Inuk hunter Ilkoo Angutikjuaq. *Photo: Debbie McAllister.*

With help from a friend, Inuk hunter Ilkoo Angutikjuaq, Siu-Ling reviewed maps and Inuit hunting routes. Together they planned and executed the logistics needed to safely navigate challenging Arctic terrain and placement of food caches along the 628-mile (1,010-kilometer) route. After some discussion, Matty arranged for Siu-Ling's dog team and Matty's own team to travel to Pangnirtung.

Twenty-four dogs in two teams driven by Matty's children, world-renowned Arctic adventurers Sarah and Eric McNair-Landry, and two other dog drivers, Willy Hyndman and Étienne Denis, began their journey from Iqaluit. They traveled across the Hall Peninsula to Pangnirtung, which Canada's *National Post* dubbed the "Switzerland of the Arctic" because of its snow-covered mountains, glacial lakes and summer wildflowers.

Arriving in Pangnirtung, which locals affectionately call "Pang," Sarah handed her teams over to Matty, who had flown ahead to Pang. After completing a distance of more than 300 miles (480 kilometers), the dogs continued on to Qikiqtarjuaq through the Pangnirtung Pass, another distance of close to 110 miles (200 kilometers), with Matty and Eric. Siu-Ling, Debbie and Connie Maley, another friend from Calgary, had flown to Qikiqtarjuaq ahead of time, and the four women — Siu-Ling, Matty, Debbie and Connie — started their journey north, to Pond Inlet, on March 31, 2009.

Toko and Rode were eight years old. While Rode was still going

Toko (far left) eventually decided he'd had enough of life as top dog. *Photo: Debbie McAllister.*

strong, Toko appeared to have a sore shoulder, possibly due to arthritis, which is not uncommon in working sled dogs. When they reached Clyde River, the two teams stopped for a couple of days to freshen up and replenish supplies before continuing to Pond Inlet, along the most isolated but spectacular parts of Baffin Island.

After their leader's departure, the team went on strike and started chewing their harnesses in protest. Matty McNair holds two of them. *Photo: Debbie McAllister.*

When the teams started getting ready to resume their journey, Siu-Ling released each dog from its tie-out chain so she could harness them one by one. As they waited their turn, they ambled around the campsite, but immediately came when called. Toko, however, decided he had had enough. He did not want to be harnessed and took off toward town. When Siu-Ling called him, he just stopped and looked at her. Although he normally would have come when called, this time he refused. He no longer wanted to be  a lead dog and rather than losing his position on the team, he decided to quit — on his own terms. The team still had more than 310 miles (500 kilometers) to travel before reaching Pond Inlet, and Siu-Ling decided not to take any chances with a dog that no longer wanted to be part of the team. After collecting Toko, Siu-Ling went into the town of Clyde River and put him on a plane back to Iqaluit. That was the end of Toko's career as a sled dog.

The two teams continued to Pond Inlet, weaving their way between hummocks, pressure ridges and leads on the sea ice, and over the bumpy, snow-covered terrain on the island.

Back in Iqaluit, Siu-Ling decided to retire Toko. He had been a hard-working and loyal sled dog, traveling thousands of kilometers on Baffin Island with her for more than eight years. Siu-Ling flew Toko to Ottawa to be neutered before we adopted him.

Toko easily adapted to life thousands of kilometers south of the Arctic. He learned to endure Ottawa's hot summers and enjoyed our daily walks on nearby forest trails and suburban streets, where he always attracted admiring glances and comments from passersby who had never seen a dog like him.

In spite of the limited time we have with retired sled dogs, they

Dog team crossing a lead, or open lane of water. *Photo: Shari Fox Gearheard.*

are a joy to have around. They mellow with age and, based on my personal experience, make good, loyal companions. They are grateful for every bit of human attention, and return it many times over. Their spine-tingling howls remind us of where they once came from. I believe it is their way to embrace us, communicate with us, sing and talk to us, as if we were one of them.

No, I have never lived in the Arctic and never managed a team of Inuit Dogs, but I had the opportunity to go dog sledding in the Arctic, help raise and train Inuit Dog puppies, and care for them in their retirement. As a librarian and researcher, I have adapted my research skills to learn more about these amazing creatures. I have also met and liaised with people involved with Inuit Dogs and the recovery of this dwindling population of dogs, formerly known as Eskimo Dogs.

The author with Toko in retirement at his new home in Ottawa. *Photo: Siu-Ling Han.*

Among them are Ken MacRury, a well-known authority on Inuit Dogs who lived in the Canadian Arctic for 30 years and wrote his master's thesis in polar studies about the Inuit Dog; Bill Carpenter, the man who established the Canadian Eskimo Dog Research Foundation with John McGrath to save and preserve the Eskimo Dog; my daughter Siu-Ling, a wildlife biologist and *qimuksiqti* ("dog teamer") who shared her love of the Inuit Dog with me, and Paul Crowley, a polar explorer and legal counsel for the Qikiqtani Inuit Association (QIA) and special legal advisor for the Qikiqtani Truth Commission (QTC). Paul and his partner, Lynn Peplinski, two seasoned dog drivers, shared their love for the Inuit Dog and their decades of experience with me. So did Matty McNair. I must not forget Sue and Mark Hamilton, who generously shared their personal photographs, their website and online journal *The Fan Hitch* (thefanhitch.org), a treasure trove of resources with its diverse mix of stories, reports and scholarly articles dedicated to the dogs and related Inuit culture.

Siu-Ling arranged for me to fly to Kimmirut, a seaside hamlet on the southwestern tip of Baffin Island, to meet Elijah and Jeannie

Padluq, well-respected Inuit elders who formerly traveled and hunted with their team of dogs. We spent a weekend with them in Elijah's hunting cabin in Qakuqtajaa. I was honored to interview these elders to learn about the time when they used to travel and hunt with dogs. I was fortunate to have the Padluqs' daughter, Kathy Martha, as interpreter and transcriber. She told me how excited her father was, and that he could not stop talking when she started asking questions about his dogs, based on a questionnaire I had prepared for her.

When Siu-Ling worked as a research assistant in Quebec's High Arctic, she fell in love with the Arctic. After graduation from the University of Waterloo, Ontario, with a master's degree in biology, Siu-Ling worked on Northern projects for the government of Canada's Northern Contaminants Program, drafting international protocols for persistent organic pollutants (POP), which are found in high concentrations in the Arctic. This protocol was an impetus for the global agreement on POPs, and the Stockholm Convention, which entered into force in 2004.

Siu-Ling never lost sight of the fact that she was living in the land of Inuit. She embraced Inuit life and culture, learned to speak Inuktitut to better communicate with Inuit hunters and elders for

Inuk elder Elijah Padluq with his daughter, Kathy Martha. *Photo: Kim Han.*

work, and started a team of traditional Inuit Dogs that she bred, raised and trained for almost two decades.

When cancer reared its ugly head once again in 2013, Siu-Ling underwent all kinds of treatments and clinical trials. Between chemo treatments she still managed to go skiing in the Rocky Mountains, as she did every February, and play ice hockey, a sport she loved since high school. Nothing was going to stop her. In between her cancer treatments, we went cross-country skiing on nearby trails every opportunity we had. Siu-Ling traveled all over Canada to visit friends and places she always wanted to see. She even undertook a 10,000-mile (16,000-kilometer) road trip out west, then south to California and back, because she wanted to see the Redwood Forest. In between she'd travel back and forth to Iqaluit to spend time in her beautiful home there, surrounded by the love and support of her many friends, the cool beauty of the Arctic, and her lovable team of dogs.

Lillian, Toko and Lao's offspring, came to live with us in Ottawa when she retired as a sled dog in 2015 at age ten. She was a great comfort to have around. Sweet Lillian never left Siu-Ling's side during Siu-Ling's last couple of weeks — it was the kind of loyalty that love stories are made of.

On her last visit to Iqaluit, in the spring of 2016, Siu-Ling was joined by her brother Jeff from Ottawa. Together they visited the dogs and went dog sledding as often as they could. After their last outing, as they were getting ready to leave, one of the dogs suddenly let out a mournful howl. He soon was joined by a chorus of his teammates, who howled with an eeriness that echoed across the frozen tundra. Jeff said it sent chills up his spine. It was as if the dogs knew they'd never see Siu-Ling again.

Siu-Ling's team.
*Photo: Fred Lemire.*

Siu-Ling shared her love and knowledge of the amazing Canadian Inuit Dog not only with me, but with the rest of the family. She was the inspiration for this book, a beacon of courage and strength who spread love and kindness all around. It is to my amazing daughter that I dedicate this book with all my love.

I am donating my income from this book to Qimmivut, a non-profit, mental-health and mentoring program for Inuit youth in Nunavut to honor Siu-Ling and the way she cared about people, the environment, Northern wildlife and her beloved Inuit Dogs.

# Introduction

Memories of an Inuk hunter

M emories of a time when his people traveled the Arctic with dogs as their most reliable companions are still vivid in the mind of 73-year-old Elijah Padluq, a well-respected Inuit elder, hunter and trapper from Kimmirut, Nunavut, Canada's northernmost territory. His bronzed, weather-beaten face creases into a smile and his eyes light up at the memory of times when he traveled and hunted with a dog team.

*Preceding page:* Copper Inuit sled near Cape Krusenstern, Northwest Territories (Nunavut). Photo by Diamond Jenness, 1915. *Courtesy Canadian Museum of History.*

*Right:* Elijah Padluq in his hunting cabin. *Photo: Kim Han.*

CANADIAN INUIT DOG

Dogs were an important part of Inuit life. Children grew up with dogs and learned to take care of them. When Elijah was young, he was given a toy sled and real puppies to play with and raise. When he was eight years old, he had between two and four dogs. He learned how to care for them and practiced running a small dog team under the watchful eye of his father. Elijah was eager to learn, and he learned quickly, taking his responsibilities very seriously. When Elijah was twelve, his father felt Elijah was ready to have his own dog team. Inuit boys who had their own small dog team and knew how to handle dogs were highly regarded and would be well respected as men.

Traveling across sea ice. *Photo: Corel.*

When Elijah grew older and got married, his wife Jeannie helped raise the dogs on his team with loving care, the way a mother raises a child. Puppies were part of the family, and newborn pups were handled and massaged in a kind of ritual that was supposed to give them certain qualities. The pups had their legs gently pulled to make them grow strong. They had their underarms rubbed and tickled so they would become more easily accustomed to the harness. They had their tails carefully twisted to curve over their backs, and some might even have their nostrils pierced with a pin to give them a good sense of smell. Inuit understood how important it was to give the dogs plenty of positive attention so they would grow into attentive,

Inuk boy training puppies, Port Burwell, Quebec, November 1927. *Source: Library and Archives Canada.*

responsive dogs, eager to work and willing to please. After all, Inuit depended on their dogs for their survival.

Elijah spent a lot of time with his dogs. He says it was important to build trust with them and to treat them well. A well-trained dog would become a very reliable and dependable helper, especially when hunting. Inuit Dogs can smell seal breathing holes and their birthing dens in the sea ice, find foxholes, and smell and hear when caribou are in the area. They sense danger and warn people when a polar bear is near, or when they are approaching thin ice. Inuit needed to be able to connect with their dogs and trust them when traveling.

"With that connection to the dogs," Elijah says, "you feel safer. Once they have traveled a route, they will never forget. If the owner isn't sure which way to go, the dogs will know, no matter how hard the owner tries to make them turn in the other

direction. When the owner is going in the wrong direction, dogs know the right direction, which way to go, and they are always right."

Inuit shared a unique bond with their dogs that went back thousands of years. Theirs was one of the world's oldest and most sophisticated human-animal partnerships. Inuit believed that part of the human race was fathered by a dog. Dogs were like family. They were the only animals to which Inuit gave names, often based on the dogs' appearances. Sometimes they were named after family members who had passed away, in which case the dogs would acquire the person's social attributes. The dogs could, therefore, be fathers, grandfathers, mothers, grandmothers, uncles or aunts to their Inuit families. The word for "dog" in Inuktitut, the language spoken by Inuit, is *qimmiq*. *Qimmiq* was not considered part of the animal kingdom. He was different from birds, insects or other mammals. *Qimmiq* was always considered in association with people. He was a vital part of Inuit existence.

Pauloosie Veevee, an Inuit elder from Pangnirtung, Nunavut, notes that in Inuit culture, a good dog team was linked to a man's masculinity. "An Inuk man was judged according to his dog team, his dogs' performance, appearance, health and endurance," he explains. If a man's dogs were obedient, happy and well fed, he was seen as a great hunter. An Inuk man who did not have a dog team was not considered a real man.

It wasn't that long ago when the survival of Inuit on the edge of the top of the world depended on *qimmiq*. As recently as the 1960s, *qimmiq* was still essential for many Inuit's semi-nomadic way of life. Together, man and dog traveled the Arctic in search of food, following the seasonal movement of the animals they hunted on land and at sea. Inuit would evaluate what their dogs

"Rough Ice." Painting courtesy of Germaine Arnaktauyok.

were doing against what they thought was the correct course of action. Many a tale has been told about the lives *qimmiq* has saved. *Qimmiq* earned himself a special place in the hearts, history, culture and traditions of Inuit, and, on May 1, 2000, the legislative assembly of the government of Nunavut, with the official herald of Canada, designated *qimmiq* as its official animal symbol and named it the Canadian Inuit Dog.

Tent house of Ikpukhuaq at Bernard Harbour, Northwest Territories (Nunavut). Rudolph Martin Anderson, 1916. *Source: Canadian Museum of History.*

While that symbolism honors the Inuit Dog's historical role in Inuit culture, many challenges lie ahead. With the arrival of snow machines, today this once-essential dog has been all but displaced in the lives of Inuit. Though tourist brochures inevitably display romantic images of sled dogs pulling passengers dressed in high-tech gear through magnificent landscapes, Inuit Dog teams are a relic of a former way of life. And, in perhaps the darkest chapters of the Inuit Dog's history, a dramatic decline in its numbers due to devastating distemper outbreaks and what was perceived as government actions threatened it with extinction.

In just a few generations, rapid technological changes have transformed Inuit from hunters and trappers living in seasonal camps to wage earners living in settlements. Nowadays, Inuit live in houses and have paying jobs. They drive motor vehicles, wear store-bought clothes, and, although they shop in supermarkets, they still value and rely on country food such as fish, caribou, seal, walrus or whale meat they gather from hunting and fishing. In spite of their changed lifestyle, the ability to travel on the land and hunt, in order to bring back food to feed their families, is a very important part of what it means to be an Inuk.

Elijah is a case in point. During summertime in his boyhood, he lived in a hide tent, and in winter his family would either build an *igloo* (snow house) or *qarmaq* (stone house) made of boulders, whale bones and sod. Today he lives in a modern house he built himself, with help from friends and family. He has running water, modern electric appliances, internet and satellite TV. There is

Igloo. *Photo: Ivan Kmit.*

no longer a team of dogs waiting restlessly in a dog yard, ready to be hitched up to go hunting. Instead Elijah travels by snow machine in winter and drives a four-wheeled ATV (all-terrain vehicle) in summer. He even has a motorboat to go fishing.

But Elijah has his memories. And in sharing them with those who are intent on learning about the Inuit Dog, he helps to ensure that these hardy dogs survive modernity as successfully as they have the freezing Arctic climate to which they are born.

# From Wolf to Dog

The Inuit Dog's transcontinental journey
from wild canid to human helpmate

People who have never seen a real Inuit Dog or wolf before might mistake the two. In his 1845 book *The History of the Dog: Its Origin, Physical and Moral Characteristics, and its Principal Varieties*, naturalist and historian William Charles Linnaeus Martin described the "Esquimaux dog," as the Inuit dog was called at the time, as "nothing more than a domesticated wolf."

Like the wolf, some Inuit Dogs can be white, black, gray or a mix of gray and brown. Inuit Dogs and wolves both have thick

*Preceding page:* Inuit Dog howling across the tundra. *Photo: Sue Hamilton.*

Arctic white wolf. *Photo: Denis Pepin.*

CANADIAN INUIT DOG

double coats and obliquely set, almond-shaped eyes that range in color from dark brown to amber to hazel. Both have triangular pointed ears that stand up straight. However, physically, wolves are generally larger, taller and heavier. They have bigger heads, and longer necks and legs. They also have bigger teeth.

In his master's thesis, *The Inuit Dog: Its Provenance, Environment and History*, Ken MacRury describes the wolf as having a "narrow, keel-like chest and forelimbs that seem pressed into the chest." In contrast, the Inuit Dog has a broad chest and a robust, muscular body built for stamina. It also has a thick neck, a wedge-shaped head and medium-length legs.

The most obvious difference is tail carriage. The Inuit Dog has a big, bushy, sickle-shaped tail carried in a tight curl over its back, especially when it is happy. The wolf has a low- and straight-hanging tail that is never curled over its back.

Inuit Dogs are said to still have one foot in the wild. They do not bark like cultured dogs, but make guttural sounds, yelping and howling like wolves. In his 1847 book *Natural History of Quadrupeds*, Scottish naturalist James Rennie writes that some of his colleagues consider these dogs "wolves in a state of

Retired Inuit sled dog. *Photo: Kim Han.*

domestication ... They never bark, but have a long, melancholy howl, like the wolf." However, Inuit Dogs can bark, although it is different from other dogs. Ken MacRury says some Inuit Dogs living south of the Arctic can bark like your neighbor's dog, but it is "learned behavior."

A 2015 study about an ancient wolf's genome in the journal *Current Biology* conducted by Pontus Skoglund, an evolutionary geneticist at Harvard's Medical School, and Love Dalén, a paleo-geneticist with the Museum of Natural History in Stockholm, traces the origin of Arctic breeds such as the Canadian and Greenlandic Inuit Dogs to a now-extinct wolf that roamed the tundra of northern Siberia some 35,000 years ago. The scientists were on an expedition on the Taimyr Peninsula in 2010, looking for Ice Age animal bones. They brought back what they thought was a reindeer rib, but DNA analysis of the two-inch-long specimen showed that it belonged to an ancient wolf.

Comparing the Taimyr wolf DNA with that of dogs and other wolves, Swedish geneticist Pontus Skoglund concluded that the ancestry of today's dogs goes back between 27,000 and 40,000 years, putting the time when wolf and dog lineages split off from each other at roughly 32,000 years ago. Skoglund found that high-latitude dogs like the Canadian Inuit Dog still retain some of the ancient Taimyr wolf's DNA.

Panorama of the Putorana plateau on Russia's Taimyr Peninsula. *Photo: Dreamstime.*

Using DNA technology, teams of international scientists in Sweden and the United States have established that dogs and wolves share the same ancestor — the ancient gray wolf, *Canis lupus*. It is believed that wolves originated in East Asia, and domesticated themselves at least 15,000 years ago, around the time when people started gathering and living in one place for the first time, creating small settlements. People living together in groups created waste that attracted scavengers such as cockroaches, rodents and, yes, wolves.

In a personal email, Peter Savolainen, world-renowned molecular biologist and associate professor of evolutionary genetics with the Royal Institute of Technology in Sweden, writes that wolves and dogs "evolved along different lines from their common ancestor ... an ancient wolf." Some of the ancient wolves' descendants continued to live in packs, wild and free, and stayed wolves. Others started frequenting human camps, even though wolves normally avoid contact with people. This line of wolves watched humans, lingering at a safe distance to sneak scraps and feast on hunters' leftovers, and eventually evolved into today's dogs, whose unique relationship with humans served an important function in the lives of the people with whom they came to live.

The forebears of today's Inuit gradually accepted the wolf into their midst, recognizing its value as an animal that could be

put to work. Over time, these animals earned their keep, were bred, and became integral to the lives of early inhabitants of the Arctic. One must imagine the challenges faced by these early hunters as they had to cover large distances on foot in search of food. They would have weighed the value of accepting these animals in their daily lives against the reality of adding more mouths to feed — a life-and-death equation. These working animals proved themselves time and again, or their presence would not have been affordable.

## Domestication

The Cambridge English dictionary defines domestication as the process of bringing animals under human control in order to provide food, power or company. In *A History of Dogs in the Early Americas*, physical anthropologist Marion Schwartz writes: "A standard definition of domestication contains two parts: a cultural component, in which humans control the breeding of the animal over which they claim ownership, and a biological component, in which an animal becomes different in form as well as behaviorally distinct from its wild ancestor."

A textbook example of domestication is the experiment by Dmitri Belyaev, a Russian geneticist who wanted to find out how domestication happens. He wanted to prove that domestication was genetically correlated to tameness. He bred silver foxes on a Siberian fur farm in Novosibirsk, selecting foxes for his experiment based on their behavior. Those that were different from their wild counterparts — less aggressive, and less fearful toward humans — became the objects of his experiment. Belyaev wanted to find out if tameness would cause the genetic changes he had seen in domesticated animals such as dogs.

For his experiment, Belyaev chose the most docile foxes at breeding time, in late January. When the cubs were old enough to breed, he would again choose the calmest among them. This breeding project, which lasted more than 40 years, eventually led to more calm and docile foxes until, after several generations, the wild foxes' behavior became like that of domestic dogs: They started wagging their tails, whimpering and whining for attention, sniffing and licking their handler's hands like dogs. They also developed floppy ears, curly tails, shorter legs and lighter coat colors.

In her paper "Early Canid Domestication. The Farm Fox Experiment," published in *American Scientist* in 1999, Lyudmilla Trut, a Russian

One of Belyaev's "mild-mannered foxes" displayed at the State Darwin Museum in Moscow. *Photo: Dreamstime.*

Charming lifesize monument to Belyaev at the Institute of Cytology and Genetics in Novosibirsk, Western Siberia. *Photo: Evgeniy Muhortov.*

geneticist who conducted the experiment with Belyaev, writes: "In the process we have observed some striking changes in physiology, morphology and behavior, which mirror the changes known in other domestic animals and bear out many of Belyaev's ideas." According to Trut, "Belyaev believed that the patterns of changes observed in domesticated animals resulted from genetic changes that occurred in the course of selection."

In their 2006 report "From Wild Wolf to Domestic Dog," published in the book *The Dog and Its Genome*, Jennifer A. Leonard, Carles Vilà and Robert K. Wayne state in capital letters: "THE DOG (*Canis familiaris*) WAS THE FIRST SPECIES to be domesticated" several thousand years ago. In his 2008 book *Dogs: Their Fossil Relatives and Evolutionary History*, Xiaoming Wang writes: "Dogs were the first animal to be fully domesticated by human hunter-gatherers, and, as such, they played a unique role in human history, instilling the idea that animals could be harnessed for human purposes."

Pack of gray wolves. *Photo: Gea Strucks.*

Scientists still have not been able to agree on where, when or how domestication first occurred. While some believe it might have been in Africa, Europe or the Middle East, the latest findings seem to point to East and Central Asia.

Wang, who is curator of vertebrate paleontology at the Natural History Museum of Los Angeles County, contends that, despite controversies about when or where dogs were first domesticated, "a general consensus exists that dogs were domesticated prior to 15,000 years before present (BP), and that domestic dogs originated in Eurasia." He mentions that "the dog was the only domesticated species that was present across Eurasia and the Americas, before the arrival of Columbus in the 15th century." Fossil evidence indicates that dogs were domesticated between 14,000 and 12,000 years ago, around the time when the first humans arrived in the New World, at the end of the last Ice Age, 15,000 years ago.

This raises several questions: Were those humans accompanied by dogs? Is there a connection between New World dogs and their Old World counterparts?

According to Robert Wayne, a professor at the University of California at Los Angeles, "Dogs are the only domesticated animals that had a New World and Old World distribution before the arrival of Columbus to North America."

To prove this, in 2002 Jennifer Leonard and her colleagues extracted DNA from the bones of 37 dog specimens from archaeological sites in Peru, Bolivia and Mexico, to ensure that no interbreeding with European dogs had occurred.

What they discovered, according to Wang, was that "native American dogs are closely related to Eurasian ancestral lineages, suggesting that dogs accompanied late Pleistocene humans when they crossed the Beringian landmass," part of which formed a land bridge that once connected Siberia and Alaska.

In a 2002 report by Leonard and Wayne in the journal *Science*, "ancient American and Eurasian domestic dogs share a common origin from Old World gray wolves. This implies that the humans who colonized America 12,000 to 14,000 years BP brought multiple lineages of domesticated dogs with them."

In his book, Wang reports that Ted Galusha, the late curator of the Frick Laboratory at the American Museum of Natural History in New York, noted that "several skulls from the late Pleistocene deposits near Fairbanks, Alaska, were extremely short-faced for wild wolves and approached the facial proportions of modern Eskimo dogs." Galusha turned his findings over to vertebrate paleontologist Stanley Olsen, who was "convinced that these fossil skulls belonged to the forerunners of Eskimo dogs."

In research published in the journal *Heredity* in 2015, Sarah Brown and fellow researchers used various DNA markers to investigate if dogs associated with Paleoeskimoes and Thule cultures arrived in the New World in two waves along with their human counterparts, or if the original Paleoeskimo dogs were founding stock for the later Thule dogs. Their findings provided "preliminary evidence that these indigenous Inuit dogs derived from ancestors brought to North America by Thule migrants from Siberia and not from the earlier dogs occasionally found with Paleoeskimo cultures," the researchers write. Referring to a 2002 paper by evolutionary biologist Jennifer Leonard, they surmise that Paleoeskimo dogs themselves may have come from earlier Native American dogs initially brought to the continent at the end of the last Ice Age, 15,000 years ago.

## Taxonomy

In spite of the thousands of years that have passed since their first association with humans, today's dogs still share the same

From left, black backed jackals; coyote; Tibetan wolf, and red fox. All are members of the same canid family. *Photos: Dreamstime.*

natural instincts as the wolf. Scientists list wolves and dogs together in the same biological family called *Canidae*, which includes coyotes, dogs, foxes, jackals and wolves.

In 1758, Swedish taxonomist Carl Linnaeus formally proposed the name *Canis familiaris* for domestic dogs.

"By and large, domestic dogs have been treated either as a species of their own, *Canis familiaris*, or as a subspecies of the gray wolf, *Canis lupus familiaris*," Wang explains in his book. In Linnaeus' famed 1758 work, *Systema Naturae*, the wolf (*Lupus*) was considered a separate genus. Wang surmises that "the fact that Linnaeus placed dog and wolf in separate genera (*Canis* and *Lupus*, respectively) perhaps implies that he did not think of any connection between the two beside their morphological similarities," which involve the external appearance and internal structure of the two animals.

In 1993, after it was established that wolves and dogs belong to the same species, W. Christopher Wozencraft, a mammologist and research scientist at the Smithsonian Institution, designated the scientific name *Canis lupus familiaris*, a subspecies of the gray wolf, for the domestic dog in his well-known book *Mammal Species of the World*.

While the Inuit Dog appears more outwardly wolf-like than the giant Great Dane or tiny Chihuahua, genetically it is not more closely related to the wolf than any other dog. Relatively few loci, or regions in the genome, control the often dramatic differences between breeds.

From Chihuahua to Dogue de Bordeaux: The plasticity of the canine genome allows for dogs of all sizes, shapes and colors. *Photo: Dreamstime.*

Although it is difficult to imagine that domestic dog breeds such as the curly-coated Poodle, long-haired Golden Retriever, flat-faced Bulldog and tiny Yorkshire Terrier are descended from the wolf, scientific evidence has established that they are. This is reflected in their scientific name, *Canis lupus familiaris*.

Going back to that now-outdated taxonomy of Linnaeus, *Canis familiaris borealis* is a subspecies designation that has been used to refer to the Eskimo Dog, now known as the Canadian Inuit Dog. The word *borealis*, affixed to the Linnean name *Canis familiaris* to describe domestic dogs, is Latin for "north." *Canis familiaris borealis* was used by the legislative assembly of the government of Nunavut to describe the Canadian Inuit Dog, which they designated as a symbol of Nunavut in 2000. It's a term that has been used in numerous articles and publications for more than a hundred years, until the name stuck.

It is, however, not considered taxonomically correct today. Calling dogs *Canis familiaris* identifies them as their own species. While the evolutionary species concept, or ESC, holds that a lineage of a particular species can diverge so significantly that it eventually can come to be considered a separate and distinct species, most experts consider the domesticated dog to simply be too young to warrant its own species name. By contrast, from a biologist's perspective, the most widely accepted views of scientific species names is the "biological species concept," or BSC, which focuses mainly on the ability to interbreed.

ITIS, or Integrated Taxonomic Information System, was established in the mid-1990s among several federal agencies to improve and expand on taxonomic data. According to ITIS, the name *Canis familiaris* is considered "invalid." There is no mention of *Canis familiaris borealis*. Although *Canis familiaris* is still widely used, the only scientific name for the domestic dog in the ITIS database is *Canis lupus familiaris*.

As far as *Canis familiaris borealis* is concerned, in many writings this scientific name for the "Esquimaux," or Eskimo Dog, is attributed to Desmarest, a disciple of Georges Léopold Nicolas Frédéric Cuvier, a professor of anatomy known as the "Father of Paleontology," later identified as Baron Cuvier.

In his 1820 book *Mammalogie en Dèscription des Èspèces des Mammifères*, Desmarest mentions *Canis familiaris borealis* and refers to Frédéric Cuvier, a celebrated naturalist, zoologist, paleontologist, and younger brother and namesake of Baron Cuvier.

In the 1844 *Encyclopaedie catholique*, Abbot Jean Baptiste Glaire writes: "Dog of the Eskimoes, *canis familiaris borealis*, another breed first described by Mr. F. Cuvier, who drew a picture of a beautiful individual that is represented in his work on mammals." Lt. Colonel Charles Hamilton Smith simply describes the Esquimaux Dog as *Canis borealis* in *The Naturalist's Library*, published in 1839. And in his *Field Notes* written in the early 1880s, field naturalist Lucien M. Turner uses the term *Canis familiaris (Linné) borealis?* — including a question mark after *borealis* — to describe the "Eskimo Dog."

Based on genetic research that you will read about in the next chapter, it would appear that Inuit and Greenland sled dogs are related to other Arctic breeds that originated in Eurasia. As a result, it would be inadvisable to consider the Canadian Inuit Dog a distinct species, because these dogs, along with their Greenland neighbors, come from an ancestor already domesticated in Eurasia.

# Ancient Beginnings

Known by many names, and a few misnomers, the Inuit Dog travels to Arctic Canada

The Canadian Inuit Dog evolved in large part by natural selection, where only the strongest survive. It is a landrace — an ancient, aboriginal population of domestic dogs that have been in Arctic Canada for more than 4,000 years.

In his paper "The Concept of an Aboriginal Breed," which appeared in The Fan Hitch in 2013, Vladimir Beregovoy, a zoologist, advisor and curator of the Russian Primitive and Aboriginal Dog Society, explains that aboriginal dogs are natural breeds. They are not like cultured breeds of domesticated animals. Aboriginal breeds "have never been developed by any planned genetic manipulation, deliberate selective breeding and intentional crossing of one breed with another." Instead, Beregovoy writes, "they are very much like wild animals, because nobody can claim authorship over any type of aboriginal dog," adding that each primitive breed has "its own unique geographic range of distribution and is always associated with a certain ethnic group."

Johan and Edith Gallant, who have been very involved in documenting the Africanis — a landrace native to southern Africa — wrote a 2010 article in The Fan Hitch entitled "Breed, Landrace and Purity: What do they mean?" In it, they note that aboriginal dog populations are a direct reflection of their native ecosystem. These dogs have adapted to their environment,

*Preceding page:*
Copper Inuit
family preparing
to leave village at
Bernard Harbour,
Northwest
Territories
(Nunavut).
Photo by John
Raffles Cox,
1915. *Courtesy
Canadian Museum
of History.*

Examples of landraces include the Indian Pariah Dog (far left) and the Armenian Gampr (center) and the Canadian Inuit Dog (right). All three developed organically, without overt interference from humans. *Photos: Sandip Mehta; Farishyan, and Kim Han.*

the Gallants write, "mostly under conditions of natural selection but, nevertheless, influenced by human preferences and interference." Aboriginal dogs are not as consistent in appearance as a more stringently bred cultured or modern breed but, according to the Gallants, they have "enough characteristics in common to permit its recognition as a group."

Inuit and their dogs depended on each other for survival in an extreme and unforgiving environment. The dogs carried packs in summer and pulled sleds in winter. Over time, they evolved physical traits that helped them survive the harsh, hostile environment in which they lived and worked: a broad, muscular chest for pulling power; small, short, furry, upright ears to withstand the extreme cold, and a long, bushy tail that they can curl over their head and nose while resting and sleeping to warm the air they breathe. They also have a dense double coat that is impervious to cold, snow and freezing rain, and thermoregulation, which will be explained in detail in a later chapter.

Not only were Inuit Dogs hunting and working companions, they also served as guardians and protectors of the humans with whom they lived. In addition to their ability to thrive and survive in extreme Arctic conditions, it was essential that they responded well to commands, and were alert and trainable.

"Dogs were a part of us," Inuit elder Elijah Padluq emphasizes. "We had to treat them with respect, treat them well. They help you, and you help them back. We had to work as a team. We used them to travel short and long distances ... they had to know you. Otherwise, they would never listen."

## Origin of the Inuit Dog

During the last Ice Age, more than 15,000 years ago, the Bering Land Bridge, or Beringia, emerged between Siberia and Alaska when sea levels dropped, linking Asia and North America. It is widely accepted that the Bering Land Bridge was the most probable migratory route of colonizers from Asia into North America.

Archaeological evidence indicates that dogs have lived in Canada's Arctic since the earliest Paleo-Inuit hunters arrived in the New World more than 4,000 years ago. Together, humans and dogs braved extreme weather and living conditions in a challenging environment where the basics of daily life were often in short supply. Their close association and ability to depend on each other became a partnership in a quest for survival that made the difference between life and death.

The Thule culture, direct ancestors of today's Inuit, developed in North America between 1,000 and 1,250 years ago. According to David Morrison and Georges Hébert-Germain of the Canadian Museum of History in Gatineau, Quebec, northern Alaska is the original homeland of Inuit culture. It was from there that the Thule spread east from Alaska, in a series of migrations between 800 and 1,000 years ago, across what is now known as the Canadian Arctic, to northwest Greenland, bringing seal-skin

The Nenets, also known as Samoyeds, are an indigenous people in northern Arctic Russia. Unlike Inuit, whose ancestors migrated from that part of the world, the Nenet do not use their dogs for pulling sledges — that role is delegated to reindeer. Instead, dogs assist with herding. *Photo: Nicholas Mayo.*

kayaks, dogs and sleds with them.

The Thule were more technologically advanced than the Paleoeskimos and Dorset, the first waves of migrants from Asia who inhabited the treeless Arctic regions of North America between 4,000 and 800 years ago. The Thule culture, also known as Neo-Inuit, used bows and arrows

Inuk woman lighting *qullig*. *Photo: Ansgar Walk.*

to hunt caribou and musk ox, and an *umiaq* (large, open seal- or walrus-skin boat) and harpoons attached to an *avatuq* (seal-skin float) to catch large sea mammals such as whales, walruses and bowhead whales (*Balaena mysticetus*). Rib bones from the bowhead whale framed summer and winter houses covered with seal skin. For insulation, Inuit used snow and sod. For heat and light, they burned *uqsuq* (fat from a sea mammal) in a shallow, hollowed stone known as *qulliq*, or "woman's lamp," using *suputiit* (a mixture of moss and Arctic cottongrass) as wicks. In a testament to their powerful spiritual bond with the land and the animals they depended on, early Inuit sometimes placed a whale skull over their house entrance to symbolize living inside the most important animal they hunted.

While some of these migrants and their dogs stayed in the Canadian Arctic, others traveled farther east to Greenland, around its entire west and east coasts, and as far south as Labrador. The dogs accompanying the Thule people to Greenland are now known as Greenland Dogs, Greenland Inuit Dogs, Greenlandic Sled Dogs or Grønlandshund.

## Brothers Across the Bay

In Greenland as in Canada, dogs were an important part of Inuit life; indeed, Greenland is considered home to the largest sled

Greenland Dogs.
Photo courtesy
Looqi Schmidt.

dog population in the Arctic region. Canadian Inuit Dogs
and Greenland Dogs are the same aboriginal landrace, although
Greenlandic Dogs can be a bit smaller, depending on the area
they came from and what they were fed.

In a September 2005 article in *The Fan Hitch*, veterinarian Hanne
Friis Andersen writes: "Greenland Dog / Canadian Inuit Dog ...
it makes no difference." She explains that the dogs the Thule
brought to Greenland around 1,000 years ago remained isolated
in the harsh Arctic environment they lived in and adapted under
conditions of natural selection. This created the type of dog that
Andersen describes as "the hard-working, healthy and strong
dog that keeps going no matter what."

Unlike Canada, Greenland prohibits the importation of any dog
to its dog-sled district, although this restriction is known to have

been violated. Dogs taken out of the country are not allowed back in to prevent contamination of the Greenland Dog. Canada has no such rules. People moving to Canada's Arctic often bring dogs with them. This has inevitably caused an increase in the number of crossbred Inuit Dogs. Matty McNair, a polar explorer and educator living in Iqaluit, fears that in another 50 years the traditional working Inuit Dog of the North may no longer exist.

(The term Northern Inuit Dog, by the way, does *not* refer to the Canadian Inuit Dog. According to the Northern Inuit Dog website at www.nisociety.com, several dogs of unspecified origin were imported from North America to Britain in the 1980s. These dogs were bred with other northern breeds such as Siberian Huskies and Alaskan Malamutes, as well as German Shepherds, "to create a wolf-look-alike dog that would be a suitable family pet and retain a willingness to work and please.")

In early 2000, the Natural History Museum of Denmark at the University of Copenhagen estimated there were around 20,000 Greenland Dogs. Ten years later, that number was reduced to 15,000. The continuing decline is attributed to climate change and increasingly shrinking sea ice due to warming air and ocean temperatures, which makes it more difficult to hunt for sea mammals. Other factors cited are the growing number of snowmobiles, fewer people using sled dogs, the cost of

Sledge dog in Illulissat, western Greenland. *Photo: Dreamstime.*

maintaining a dog team, and the rising cost of commercial dog food, as Inuit cannot always depend on country food from hunting and fishing to feed their dogs.

In 2014, the Greenland Dog was recognized as a distinct breed by the Fédération Cynologique Internationale (FCI), the world's largest dog organization, which classifies it amid the "Spitz and Primitive Types." Denmark has been given the authority to control the standard of the Greenland Dog (Grønlandshund in Danish). The FCI standard refers to it as "one of the world's oldest breeds," adding that, since ancient times, it has been "the Inuits' [sic] only sledge dog."

However, the FCI fails to mention the Canadian Inuit Dog, even though these dogs had been in the Canadian Arctic before there were any in Greenland!

## The Canadian Eskimo Dog

For its part, the Canadian Inuit Dog is recognized by the Canadian Kennel Club (CKC), which still refers to it, formally, as the Canadian Eskimo Dog. However, all the official-looking pedigrees are of little concern to Inuit and non-Inuit who are breeding working dogs. They are less concerned about the dogs' external appearance than whether or not they have the strength and endurance to be good working dogs that can thrive and survive in the harsh and unforgiving Arctic.

Andrew Maher, a resource conservation manager working for the government of Canada in Nunavut, has owned a dog team for years. He writes that he does not know any Canadian Inuit Dog owners in Nunavut who register their dogs with the Canadian Kennel Club. The kennel club is more interested in show dogs, he explains, while "most team owners are more interested in making sure that the breed survives as a working dog."

All in all, there are more Inuit Dogs (also known as Inuit Sled Dogs) in Canada than the number of these dogs that are registered as "Canadian Eskimo Dogs" by the CKC.

Canadian Eskimo Dogs that are part of an official kennel-club registry are bred to a written standard based on appearance. Most are bred and raised in kennels south of the treeline. By comparison, in  the treeless Arctic, Matty McNair says, "a good sled dog that is required to run in a fan hitch, as a member of a pack, needs to be raised as a pack dog so it can learn the rules."

Canadian Eskimo Dog enthusiasts should be acknowledged for their effort to preserve this unique breed by ensuring that their

Canadian Eskimo Dog Champion Torch (left), foundation bitch for the Arctic Ice kennel in Fort Assiniboine, Alberta, Canada, with her daughter Gjoa. *Photo: Brianna Olesen.*

Canadian Eskimo Dogs winners who competed at a specialty show for indigenous Canadian breeds. *Photo courtesy Bevereley Arseneau.*

dogs emulate their brothers in the North. Beverly Arseneau of Arctic Ice Kennels, a breeder of Canadian Eskimo Dogs in Fort Assiniboine, Alberta, downplays differences between Inuit Dogs born, raised and working in the Arctic and those south of the treeline: "Moving south of 60 [a reference to the 60th parallel] does not instantly change thousands of years of genetic evolution and development. Many of the dogs south of 60 are in working homes where the dogs are working distances, working trap lines, working tours, accumulating 350+ miles a month on tours alone ...."

While there is no doubt Canadian Eskimo Dogs born, raised and working south of the treeline in temperatures that can dip to -40° Fahrenheit ( -40° Celsius) work just as hard as their brothers in the North, it would be interesting for a comparative study to be done on their physical strength, resilience and stamina. Would an "Eskimo Dog" born and brought up south of the treeline survive traveling a minimum of 40 miles (65 kilometers) during the course of one day — day after day — to complete an average distance of approximately 250 miles (400 kilometers) within one week, like the dogs on the Pangaggujjiniq Nunavut

Quest, where there is no sophisticated support system or veterinary medical presence? Or the dogs on the Ivakkak Sled Dog Race, which covers an average distance of 372 miles (600 kilometers) within seven to ten days? Has a comparative study been done on the physiology, muscle mass, hardiness and endurance of these dogs, and the way they were bred, trained and reared?

While the American Kennel Club does not recognize the Canadian Eskimo Dog, the Kennel Club in Great Britain does. Here, Napu of Northwinds at Akna, who descends from purely working lines in Nunavut, competes in the Working Group at the famous Crufts dog show in 2016. *Photo by Boris Glukhareb, courtesy Racheal Bailey.*

Inuit Dogs living and working in the Arctic are tough and resilient. Vladimir Beregovoy considers them "natural monuments of nature and culture, because they have proven their usefulness and passed the test of time." He comments on the radical changes of the late 19th Century, when dogs were bred pure with pedigree records and used for show contests:

"The best dogs suitable for breeding should not be show champions, but rather best-rated dogs," he wrote. "Entire dog shows and trials of aboriginal breeds should be redesigned to emphasize field behavior and physical performance … Using and breeding aboriginal dogs for performance of a different job that is new to them would change them, especially if they were selected for greater trainability."

The Canadian Inuit Dogs website (www.canadianinuitdogs.com) was created and managed by Debora Segna and Fabrizio Giammateo, two devoted "Canadian Inuit (Eskimo) Dog" enthusiasts living in Italy. This website posts a database of Canadian Inuit (Eskimo) Dogs living in Canada, the United States and Europe. As of 2014, their database listed 333 Inuit Dogs, of which 269 were in Canada.

According to the Canadian Eskimo Dog website (www.CanadianEskimoDog.com), as of 2016 there were 279 registered Canadian Eskimo Dogs in Canada. In a 2018 email, the Canadian Kennel Club indicates that the number of Canadian Eskimo Dogs it has registered to date is 197, 82 less than two years ago. With a few exceptions, neither number includes Inuit Dogs bred as working dogs by Northerners — that is, Inuit and non-Inuit in Canada's Northwest Territories, Nunavut and Nunavik.

In Beregovoy's opinion, saving aboriginal dogs in their countries of origin is the most reliable way of securing the survival of these unique dogs. But while Inuit Dogs have maintained their indigenous nature, the same can't be said of their numbers: In the early 1900s, there were an estimated 20,000 Inuit Dogs in Canada's Arctic. By the 1970s, according to the Canadian Kennel Club, that number had nosedived to 200. This was due in large part to the introduction of snowmobiles, which were faster, could travel farther, and required less care than a dog team. Other contributing factors included infectious diseases that decimated thousands of Inuit Dogs and, as in Greenland, shrinking sea ice, which made it more difficult to hunt sea mammals. Other mitigating factors were the time and cost of maintaining a team, as well as what was a dark moment in the history of the Canadian Inuit Dog, described in a later chapter.

According to Harry Okpik, a champion dog musher from Nunavik, he and his fellow dog sledders have been breeding Inuit Dogs to try to get back what Okpik calls the Eskimo Husky. "It takes a long time to get the purity that you want in a husky," he explains, "but it is slowly starting to show."

Nonetheless, simple demographics suggest that, as modernity continues to whittle away at traditional Inuit life, so too does it threaten the dogs that have been at their side for millennia.

## What's In a Name?

Before the legislative assembly of the government of Nunavut

Alaskan Malamute. *Photo: Dreamstime.*

Siberian Husky. *Photo: Dreamstime.*

selected *qimmiq* to be the official animal symbol of Nunavut in 2000 and named it the Canadian Inuit Dog, the Inuit Dog was also known as Canadian Eskimo Dog. According to wildlife biologist Bill Carpenter's research, the Canadian Eskimo Dog had been recognized by the Canadian Kennel Club since 1891 and had been known by several names, including Eskimo Sledge Dog, Esquimaux Dog, Esquimaux Husky, Husky and Eskimo. People also called it Inuit Sled Dog, Inuit Husky, Husky Dog and Eskimo Husky.

But the Canadian Inuit Dog should not be confused with the more common and better-known huskies such as the Siberian Husky and Alaskan Malamute.

Like the Inuit Dog, those Arctic dogs belong to the spitz family. They have similar double coats; upright, pointy ears; almond-shaped eyes, and bushy tails they carry in a curl over their backs. Although to the untrained eye, the Inuit Dog, Alaskan Malamute and Siberian Husky appear to resemble each other, they are not the same dog. In fact, the Inuit Dog predates them all.

Dogs that were thought to be Inuit Dogs were brought to Wonalancet, New Hampshire, to Chinook kennels owned by Milton and Eva "Short" Seeley, where they were used to create a breed the Seeleys christened the Alaskan Malamute. But DNA tests of Malamutes, Siberian Huskies and Inuit Dogs show those dogs are genetically different.

"Malamute" was a generic term for just about any polar spitz dog, originating from the Mahlemiut, a regional group of Eskimos of Northwest Alaska. White people who came to the region referred to the dogs of the Mahlemiut as "malamutes," and the name stuck and generalized.

"Husky" is a generic or common name for any northern breed of sled dog, not a specific breed. The term husky is commonly used to describe any polar spitz-type dog that pull sleds.

According to Carpenter, Inuit also used the English word "Husky" for their dogs. He explains the word evolved from "Eskimo," which describes the aboriginal inhabitants of the Arctic coastal regions of northeastern Siberia, Alaska, Canada and Greenland. In the Arctic, Eskimo Sledge Dogs or Eskimo Dogs became known as Eskie Dogs, which evolved to Eskies, then Uskies, and finally Huskies or Husky Dogs. Carpenter notes a related use of this word occurred when the first Siberian dogs were brought to Alaska in the early 1900s. Initially called the Siberian Uskie, the breed quickly came to be called the Siberian Husky.

In 1854, Mgr. Alexandre Taché, bishop of St. Boniface, Manitoba, explained that the name "Esquimaux" was derived from the Cree word *Ayaskimew*. The meaning of the name is found in its two roots: *aski* (raw flesh, or fish) and *mitsow* (he eats) — implying "He who eats raw flesh or fish." The name "Eskimo" is, therefore, derogatory, although "Eskimo" is still considered acceptable among Alaska natives of Yupik and Iñupiaq heritage.

Today, native inhabitants of the Canadian Arctic are called Inuit, whereas Inuit in Greenland consider themselves Greenlanders.

After the name Inuit became the official term to describe "Eskimos," requests were made to the Canadian Kennel Club to change the name of the Canadian Eskimo Dog to Canadian Inuit Dog, but the process is a long one, requiring approval from the breed and kennel clubs as well as the government. However, some have started using the name Canadian Eskimo/Inuit Dog.

Purely Inuit, and south of the border: A retired Inuit Dog. *Photo: Kim Han.*

CANADIAN INUIT DOG

## "Real Huskies"

Inuit are very much aware of the different kinds of huskies we see today. To Inuit, *qimmiq* is the only real husky. "Real huskies" are aboriginal dogs, dogs of the past, "dogs of our ancestors," dogs that have not changed in appearance, function or temperament in more than a thousand years, although they may differ in size depending on where they live, and what they are fed. Dogs fed seal, whale and walrus grow bigger than dogs reared on caribou or fish, which aren't as rich and nutritious.

"They were real huskies — my dad's dogs — real huskies," explained an Inuk in Coral Harbour interviewed in 1997 by anthropologist Kerrie Ann Shannon of the University of Fairbanks in Alaska. "They were bigger and more powerful – bigger than the dogs we usually see here."

"Real huskies are much stronger," concurs Inuk elder Elijah Padluq. "They are calmer. Not as wild as mixed breeds. Real huskies are always eager to work pulling sleds. They travel with you mostly everywhere you go, either as a team or one dog going with you."

In a 2005 interview in *The Fan Hitch*, Daniel Annanack, a teacher at the Ulluriaq School in Kangiqsualujjuaq, Nunavik, remembered that "the pure dogs from when I was young are different from the dogs we have now. Many dogs in town are mixed from other dogs. The pure Inuit Sled Dogs are tougher dogs, and they are better for pulling sleds. The mixed dogs we have now get tired faster and are often hurting the pads of their feet."

Annanack found mixed breeds were less obedient and more aggressive than pure Inuit Dogs. "When the owner gets mad at pure sled dogs, the dogs don't get mad at the owner," he said. "The dogs we have now, when you get mad at them, they get mad at you."

## Consulting the DNA

Canadian Inuit Dogs, Greenland Dogs, Canadian Eskimo Dogs ... Can this geographically diffused population of dog still be considered one breed, however loosely one defines that term?

In her 2005 master's thesis, *Population Genetic Analysis of the Greenland Dog and Canadian Inuit Dog – Is It the Same Breed?* Hanne Friis Andersen concludes that, based on mitochondrial DNA collected from blood samples, "there is no genetic evidence of significant difference between Canadian Inuit Dogs and Greenland Dogs ... they are populations of the same breed."

In a 2013 report that appeared in the *Journal of Archaeological Science*, Sarah Brown, a researcher in anthropology and veterinary genetics at the University of California at Davis, and her colleagues compared the genetic profiles of 100- to 800-year-old archaeological samples recovered from western Alaska and northwestern Greenland with those of modern Inuit

Sled Dogs. The objective was to find out if there was "genetic continuity between dogs of the Thule [the ancestors of today's Inuit] and Inuit and, more recently, whether genetic ancestry has been replaced by post-colonial European breeds."

Brown and her colleagues analyzed 21 samples of canine skeletal remains that predate the arrival of Europeans, and three "post-contact dog skeletal remains" from three different Arctic locations. The mitochondrial DNA of these samples was compared to a collection of 51 modern Canadian Inuit and Greenland Inuit Sled Dogs, and 26 Alaskan Malamutes to determine the ancestry of both the archeological and modern dogs. The ancient samples from Alaska and Greenland, and modern genetic sequences from Greenland, all contained a high frequency of a gene sequence called "A31," which, according to Brown, was only found in modern North American Arctic dogs.

However, only one of the 26 Alaskan Malamutes tested possessed the A31 haplotype (a group of genes inherited

Canadian Inuit Dogs from Lee Inuaraq's team taking part in the 2017 Nunavut Quest. *Photo: Clare Kines.*

Canadian Inuit Dog. *Photo: Kim Han.*

together from a single parent), implying that the A31 haplotype "is not a common one in the Malamute breed." Instead, the most common sequence in the Alaskan Malamute is haplotype A29, which is also quite common among the Siberian and Alaskan huskies, another relatively modern Arctic breed.

Based on this unique A31 haplotype, Sarah Brown argues that Inuit Dogs from Canada and Greenland are the same aboriginal landrace. This specific group of genes is unique for both populations, and allows scientists to trace their origins back to indigenous dogs in the North American Arctic 600 and 700 years ago, long before European colonization.

Greenland Dog. *Photo: Mogens Trolle.*

This is corroborated by Barbara van Asch and other researchers in their 2013 paper *Pre-Columbian origins of Native American dog breeds, with only limited replacement by European Dogs, confirmed by mtDNA analysis.* "Inuit Sled Dogs, Canadian Eskimo Dogs and Greenland Dogs had similar mtDNA gene pools," they conclude. What is interesting about this statement is that they mention "Inuit Sled Dogs, Canadian Eskimo Dogs and Greenland Dogs," as if they were three different breeds, when they actually are the same breed, although they later noted that "in accordance with the mtDNA data, [these dogs] are often considered a single breed and are thought to descend from sled dogs bred by Thule people, the ancestors of the modern Inuits."

Van Asch and her colleagues confirmed that the most frequent haplotype for Inuit Sled Dogs, Canadian Eskimo Dogs and Greenland Dogs was A31, a haplotype that is unique to them. Another haplotype that is unique to the Inuit and Greenland dogs is A124.

All proof that these now geographically separated branches of this Arctic dog family are as similar on the inside as they are on the outside.

Canadian Eskimo Dog. *Photo courtesy Beverley Arseneau.*

# On the Outside

A number of physical traits helps the Inuit Dog
survive the relentlessly frigid Arctic

As a result of geographic isolation prior to European contact, the traditional Inuit Dog, or *qimmimmarit* in Inuktitut, has not changed much over the thousands of years since it first arrived in Canada's North. Unlike other domesticated dogs that were bred and crossbred, trained and conditioned to create the modern breeds we know today, the Canadian Inuit Dog is a primitive aboriginal dog, a unique and hardy race that is superbly adapted to Arctic weather, living and working conditions.

*Preceding page:* Inuit Dogs on Baffin Island running in a fan hitch. *Photo: Shari Fox Gearheard.*

A male Inuit Dog (standing) with a visible ruff. His female counterpart does not have this prominent growth of fur around the neck. *Photo: Siu-Ling Han.*

# APPEARANCE

## Coat

Inuit Dogs have a thick, double coat. The outer coat, which is stiff and straight, is called guard hair. It has an oily, waterproof coating that protects the animal from rain and snow. Under the guard hair is a soft, dense, woolly undercoat that keeps the dog warm and dry in very cold temperatures. The Inuit Dog has a mane-like growth of fur around his neck that sticks down and outward from below his ears. This is especially noticeable in males and is an example of sexual dimorphism, a phenotypic difference between males and females of the same species. This mane-like ruff is approximately three to five inches (seven to 15 centimeters) long. It gives the impression that the Inuit Dog is bigger than it actually is and helps protect its neck in fights.

Some Inuit Dogs have thick fur on their haunches that makes them look as if they are wearing bloomers. Inuit Dogs born with an excessively long, silky coat that is different from their littermates are known as *merqujuk*. In his master's thesis, Ken MacRury writes that the occurrence of *merqujuk* puppies, which

Merqujuk youngster with abnormally long coat. *Photo courtesy of Sue and Mark Hamilton.*

*Merqujuk puppy with its conventionally coated littermates. Photo courtesy of Sue and Mark Hamilton.*

is caused by a low-frequency recessive gene, is unpredictable. In a team of working dogs, such a coat is undesirable because it provides little protection against the weather. In a snowstorm, snow sticks to it. The warmth of the dog's body melts the snow and turns it into clumps of ice that cling to the fur. *Merqujuk* puppies in working teams are often destroyed at birth. Others are raised for their fur to trim Inuit clothing.

Tivi Etok, an Inuit elder who was interviewed in 2006 by Mark Brazeau of Kangiqsualujjuaq, Nunavik, said: "Sometimes dogs even had fur that would touch the ground. Those dogs that were really furry would get their fur tangled often, even in the ropes. The dogs with long, wavy fur were not good dogs."

## Color

The range of coat color in Inuit Dogs includes creamy white, white, gray, brown, buff, black, cinnamon and rust, in all kinds of shades and variations. No particular color or color pattern predominates among Inuit Dogs. Some have white bodies with patches of black, brown, red or cinnamon on the body, or

around their eyes and ears. Others are predominantly black or
dark gray with a white underbody and white markings on the
face, chest, legs, tail and feet. Inuit Dogs born in the same litter
typically have different colors and markings. One pup may be
almost pure white or all white with mask-like markings, while
its littermate might be white with random brown, rust or black
patches on its body. Other siblings might be black, red, buff,
cinnamon or gray with white underbodies and legs. Some are a
silvery white with gray tips that make them look as if they have a
dusting of gray on their backs.

Color and pattern do not define the Inuit Dog. What is important
to Inuit is what MacRury describes as the "protective qualities"
of the Inuit Dog's coat in an Arctic environment.

An Inuit Dog with a colored head can have white spots above
the eyes that look like a second pair of eyes. Inuit call them

Newborn puppies
demonstrating
the variety of coat
colors that can be
present in a single
litter. *Photo: Siu-
Ling Han.*

Inuit Dogs retracing the Qitdlarssuaq migration, March 1987-May 1988. *Photo: Mike Beedell.*

Inuit dogs have coats that are two colors. *Photo: Debbie McAllister.*

Five-week-old puppy with *taqulik*, or lighter-colored spots above his eyes. *Photo: Siu-Ling Han.*

CANADIAN INUIT DOG

*taqulik*. They are particularly striking in black-headed dogs and make them look fierce. Not all Inuit Dogs have *taqulik*.

## Eyes

An Inuit Dog has almond-shaped, obliquely set eyes that come in different shades of dark brown and amber, depending on its pigment. Inuit Dogs are born with dark blue or mauve eyes that change color as they grow older. Adult Inuit Dogs never have blue eyes, which would be an indication of contamination with the genes of another breed.

Siberian Husky with blue eyes, which are a sign of crossbreeding in Inuit Dogs. *Photo: Dreamstime.*

In his 2002 article "Blue Eyes in Norway's Greenland Dogs," Ove Nygaard, a longtime Inuit Dog owner and breeder in Norway, argues that blue eyes were never part of the Inuit Dog gene pool, suggesting that crosses with Siberian Huskies and subsequent inbreeding brought it to the fore in certain lines.

Inuit Dogs can have pigment that is either black or brown, as with this dog. *Photo: Shari Fox Gearheard.*

A potful of puppies. *Photo: Siu-Ling Han.*

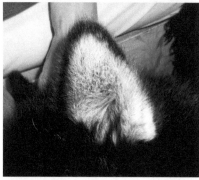

Inuit Dog's ear. *Photo: Kim Han.*

A broken ear that was damaged in a dog fight. *Photo: Siu-Ling Han.*

Inuit Dogs have either black or brown eye rims and lips, depending on their pigment.

## Ears

An Inuit Dog is born with tiny ears that are folded flat forward but stand up straight within days. As the puppy grows and develops his hearing, this allows him to move his ears to catch sounds much farther away than a human can hear. The short, triangular ears with rounded tips are thick and furry to prevent frostbite. True Inuit Dogs never have floppy ears. A floppy ear on an Inuit Dog, except when it has been broken in a fight, is considered a defect and a sign that it has been contaminated with another breed.

## Size and Substance

The Inuit Dog is a moderately sized dog with a powerful build. He has a thick neck with a wedge-shaped head, broad shoulders, and a broad, well-muscled chest for pulling power. Inuit Dogs have a level topline. Their height at the withers (top of the shoulder) and hips is almost equal. Depending on its function, environment and diet, the average male Inuit Dog is 23 to 27½ inches (58 to 70 centimeters) at the withers and weighs between 66 and 83 pounds (30 to 38 kilograms).

Just because a dog is bigger does not necessarily mean he is stronger or faster. The average female Inuit Dog is considerably smaller and finer boned. Females weigh an average of 59 pounds (26.8 kilograms) and are between 22 and 24 inches (55 to 61 centimeters) tall.

Example of a correct topline: level and strong, never sloping or sagging. *Photo: Kim Han.*

## Legs and Feet

Inuit Dogs have webbed feet, long, strong nails, and fur between their toes for gripping icy surfaces. The pads of their feet are tough to enable them to run for miles on rough terrain. Inuit Dogs can have pink or black foot pads.

Johnny-George Annanack, an 85-year-old elder from Kangiqsualujjuaq, Nunavik, believes that dogs with black pads have tougher feet. Unlike light-colored pads, black pads do not get cut as easily in the spring. Some dog-team owners put booties on their dogs' feet to protect them from the sharp, icy pinnacles that form in the pools of melt water on top of the sea ice in the spring, when the snow melts during the day and freezes overnight. Others do not use booties to toughen the dogs' feet in the springtime.

The Inuit Dog's elbows turn outward, giving him an almost bow-legged but sturdy appearance. Like wolves, Inuit Dogs are digitigrades: They stand, walk and run on their toes. Their toes grip and cling to rocks, making it possible for them to accelerate their pace and achieve astonishing bursts of speed when chasing prey. Their long toes also enable them to run on uneven terrain. Inuit Dogs do not have rear dewclaws.

Most four-legged animals have four working gaits. What is

unique about the Inuit Dog is that it has five. In addition to the walk (four-beat gait), canter/lop (three-beat gait), trot (two-beat gait) and gallop (four-beat gait), the Canadian Inuit Dog also paces. A trot is a two-beat gait in

An Inuit Dog's furry foot. *Photo: Kim Han.*

which two diagonal legs move in unison. In a pace, two lateral legs move forward together. That means that the feet on the same side are lifted and put down together.

According to Harry Okpik, a champion dog musher who has participated in at least ten Ivakkak dog-sled races, dogs using a four-beat gait "move faster, and they don't get tired faster."

Dogs working near Kulusuk village in Greenland. The dog in the foreground at left is a perfect example of the pace, a four-beat gait that is very effective at conserving energy. *Photo: Pavel Svoboda.*

# On the Inside

Hard-wired instinct makes the Inuit Dog an
indispensible human partner in polar survival

The previous chapter discussed the physical traits that make the Inuit Dog so well suited to its environment and its work. Some of these aspects of structure help give the Inuit Dog the strength and resilience needed to negotiate a most inhospitable climate. But there are other, less tangible factors — such as genetics and rearing — that are just as important in ensuring this native dog's survival.

## Strength

The Inuit Dog is a superb working animal that played an indispensable role in Inuit culture. Inuit Dogs can travel up to 65 miles (100 kilometers) a day or more, pulling a heavily loaded *qamutiik*, day after day. Living up to the nickname of the "pulling machine of the North," each dog can pull up to twice his weight, or approximately 176 pounds (80 kilograms), depending on the terrain traveled.

In her paper *The Dogs of the Inuit: Companions in Survival*, Lynn Peplinski of the Inuit Heritage Trust in Nunavut retells Ken MacRury's story about Tatigat, an Inuk hunter who crossed Hecla and Fury Straits in 1975 with his 14-dog team after a month of hunting. MacRury was out caribou hunting near the Baffin Island

*Preceding page: Keeping warm under a blanket of snow. Photo: Debbie McAllister.*

site with his friend Attagutalaqkutuq when he met Tatigat, who
was on his way to Igloolik with his family.

MacRury and Attagutalaqkutuq helped Tatigat turn his sled to
ice its runners. On Tatigat's four-foot-by-21-foot (1.2-meter-by-
6.5-meter) *qamutiik* were 14 frozen caribou carcasses, more than
30 dried seal skins and a number of wadded tarpaulins. Atop
all that, Tatigat had caribou sleeping skins, two wooden boxes
filled with tools, pots and pans, two steamer trunks and two
whole seals he had caught en route. In front of this load he had
a washtub lined
with a large
caribou-hide
bag containing
five puppies.
Tatigat's wife
carried a
small child in
her *amautik*
(hooded parka).
Their two
children under
ten years of age
were also on
the *qamutiik*.
Together they

Woman carrying
toddler in *amautik*.
Photo: Debbie
McAllister.

had traveled across flat sea ice, pulled by a team of 14 dogs over
a distance of 80 miles (130 kilometers) in about 17 hours. The
temperature was -22° Fahrenheit (-30° Celsius). It was estimated
that each dog pulled around 220 pounds (100 kilograms).

Following Tatigat were his son and daughter (10 and 15 years
old) traveling on an almost 10-foot (three-meter) long *qamutiik*
pulled by a team of five dogs. The *qamutiik* was loaded with the
children and 286 pounds (135 kilograms) of caribou antlers that
were to be sold to the Hudson Bay store.

In his book *Fauna Boreali-Americana (The Zoology of the*

*Northern Parts of British America; Containing Descriptions of
the Late Northern Land Expedition, under Command of Captain
Sir John Franklin)*, Scottish naturalist and Arctic explorer Sir John
Richardson wrote about 19th-Century British explorer Captain
George Francis Lyon, commander of the Hecla, one of the ships
that took part in the 1821-1823 expedition to find the Northwest
Passage that was led by Captain William E. Parry. When their
ships were trapped in sea ice in Repulse Bay, on the shore of
Hudson Bay, Lyon met Inuit and their dog teams, who taught
him Arctic survival skills, hunting and traveling by dog sled.
During that time, Lyon had many opportunities to observe and
study the "Eskimaux's" dogs.

In his *Private Journal*, published in 1825, Lyon described the
dogs of the "Eskimaux" as "useful creatures being indispensable

Inuit igloo village
by George Francis
Lyon. *From "The
Private Journal
of Captain G. F.
Lyon of H.M.S.
Hecla during the
recent Voyage of
Discovery under
Captain Parry,"
published 1824.*

attendants on the Eskimaux." He described how pups were
trained to become sled dogs:

"Young dogs are put into harness as soon as they can walk, and
being tied up, soon acquire a habit of pulling, in their attempts
to recover their liberty, or roam in quest of their mother. When
about two months old, they are put into the sledge with the
grown dogs, and sometimes eight or ten little ones are under

the charge of some steady old animal, where with frequent and sometimes cruel beatings, they soon receive a competent education. Every dog is distinguished by a particular name, and the angry repetition of it has an effect as instantaneous as application of the whip."

Lyon later bought a team of 11 "very fine animals" and learned to drive them, to see how well they did as draft animals. After several experiments he found that three of his dogs could pull him on a sledge weighing 100 pounds (45.35 kilograms) over a distance of one mile (1.6 kilometers) in six minutes. To prove the strength of "a well-grown dog," his lead dog alone could pull a load of 196 pounds (89 kilograms), the same distance, in eight minutes.

"At another time," he wrote, "seven of my dogs ran a mile in four minutes 30 seconds, drawing a heavy sledge full of men. I stopped to time them; but had I ridden, they would have gone equally fast; in fact I afterwards found that ten dogs took five minutes to go over the same space. Afterwards, in carrying stores to the Fury, one mile distant, nine dogs drew 1611 pounds (730.737 kilograms) in the space of nine minutes!"

Lyon professed his admiration for "Eskimaux dogs" and apologized for the frequency with which he referred to them:

"Whoever has had the patience to read this account, will laugh at my introducing my team so frequently in a professed account of Eskimaux dogs generally; but I can only offer as my excuse, the merits of my poor animals, with which I have often, with one or two persons besides myself, on the sledge returned home from the Fury, a distance of near a mile, in pitchy darkness, and amidst clouds of snow drift, entirely under the care of those trusty servants who, with their noses down to the snow, have galloped on board entirely directed by their sense of smelling. Had they erred, or been at all restive, no human means could have brought us on board until the return of clear weather."

# Endurance

The Inuit Dog is also known for his endurance. In 2007 and 2009, Nadine Gerth, a biologist at the Ludwig Maximilian University in Munich, Germany, and her team examined the physiology of Inuit Sled Dogs in Greenland under the direction of Professor J.M. Starck. They studied the way the dogs adapt to extreme and seasonal fluctuations in their natural environment and living conditions, and how their bodies adjust to changes in temperature, exercise and food supply.

Winter is the dogs' working season, when they are regularly fed high-quality meats such as whale, walrus and seal. In summer and fall, their inactive period, the dogs are chained outside villages and are only given low-quality food such as fish, once or twice a week. Sometimes they don't have anything to eat for prolonged periods of time.

Gerth and her team compared the physiology of active and inactive dogs and how the dogs adjust to increased workload at the end of their inactive period.

"Inuit Sled Dogs switch from resting to heavy work without an obvious training period," they write. "In contrast, human athletes would have to train for weeks when aiming to reach a similar level of performance as Inuit sled dogs, during the winter." Inactive dogs were often heavily infested with intestinal parasites; endoscopic exams of the same dogs in winter found hardly a single worm, even though the dogs were not given any parasiticides.

The Inuit Dogs' strength and endurance have been legendary throughout history. In one of the earliest polar migrations by Inuit, Qitdlarssuaq — also known as Qillarsuaq or Qillaq, a respected and feared Inuit leader and *angakkuq* (shaman) from Baffin Island — led a band of approximately 50 North Baffin Inuit to northwest Greenland in the mid-1800s. In a section that appeared in the *Canadian Encyclopedia*, John Bennett recounts

CANADIAN INUIT DOG

how Qitdlarssuaq and his band traveled from Cumberland Sound in the southeast of Baffin Island to an area near Pond Inlet in North Baffin. They continued across Lancaster Sound to Devon Island in Baffin Bay, where they stayed several years, before continuing along the coast of Ellesmere Island, the most northerly island in Canada's Arctic, to northwest Greenland. They carried all their possessions, including kayaks, by dog sled. It took them more than a decade to move more than 2,000 miles (3,200 kilometers) from Cumberland Sound to northwest Greenland, where they arrived in Pitorarvik around 1863.

Inuit Dogs can vary significantly in size, color and appearance. But what they all share is the ability to survive in their uniquely harsh environment.
*Photo: Clare Kines.*

More than a century later, in 1987, teacher, wildlife technician and wilderness guide Renee Wissink retraced the Qitdlarssuaq migration, traveling more than 1,700 miles (2,736 kilometers) from Igloolik to Pond Inlet, then north, to Qanaaq, Greenland. Wissink was accompanied by four men: Paul Apak, Theo Ikummaq, Mike Immaroitak and Mike Beedell, an adventurer and photographer from Chelsea, Quebec. They traveled with 46 purebred Eskimo sled dogs divided into three teams from mid-March 1987 until mid-May, 1988.

Another example of the Inuit Dog's strength and legendary endurance are the Inuit Dogs on the 1986 unsupported trek to

Inuit Dog asleep in the snow. *Photo: Debbie McAllister.*

the North Pole led by Will Steger of Minnesota. The team was made up of 49 dogs, of which 19 were Inuit Dogs. The rest were dogs that were crossbred with Alaskan Huskies for speed.

Brent Boddy, one of the expedition members on that North Pole trek, described the dogs' role in a personal email in 2006. "In the initial stage of the expedition during the first three weeks when conditions were at the harshest, the teams made up mostly of Inuit dogs kept the expedition moving, because the Inuit dogs were more suited to the severe cold and heavy loads," he explains. "Loads were relayed by doing two trips and, on several days during this period, only the Inuit Dog teams did the second trip. On the last half of the expedition, when temps were warmer and the loads lighter, the crossbred dogs excelled because they kept a faster pace than the Inuit Dogs which helped to cover greater distances. So you could say that the two types of dogs (crossbreds and Inuit Dogs) complimented each other in obtaining the Pole unsupported."

According to Boddy, the Inuit Dogs proved they had better endurance. They also did much better in the cold.

CANADIAN INUIT DOG

In the winter of 1990, Swiss musher and polar adventurer Markus Bischoff used Inuit Dogs from Greenland and Canada to mush from Yellowknife, Northwest Territories, to Cape Columbia on Ellesmere Island, completing a remarkable distance of 2,485 miles (4,000 kilometers). Bischoff was the first to cross the Canadian Arctic from south to north by dog team.

## Resilience

Inuit Dogs are among the world's toughest domestic animals. Over thousands of years, the Inuit Dog has proven that life in polar climates depended on survival of the fittest.

Inuit Dogs can survive a raging Arctic blizzard with no extra protection. They do not need shelter to protect them from the elements. These dogs are known to be able to subsist on very little food.

In his thesis, MacRury refers to a 1988 report by David Mech, a wolf expert, in which dogs had been "starved experimentally for as long as 116 days" and were still able to recover. He also quotes zoologist Magnus Degerbøl and writer-explorer Peter Freuchen, who in 1935 refer to the Inuit Dog as having "a tremendous capacity for tolerating hunger and cold."

"These are the dogs that can survive up here," McNair says. "If you run out of food, they keep going. They're just tough as nails."

In his *Private Journal*, Captain Lyon wrote about an excursion he took with his dog team: "Our dogs had eaten nothing for 48 hours, and could not have gone over less than 70 miles of ground. Yet they returned, to all appearance, as fresh and active as when they first set out."

MacRury states that the Inuit Dog possesses "exceptional

recuperative powers from wounds and injuries." According to Paul Crowley, a polar explorer and longtime Inuit Dog owner living in Iqaluit: "If they can lick their wounds, they will not become infected."

The most common cause of injury to Inuit dogs is fighting among themselves. It does not take much for Inuit Dogs to get into a fight. The alpha dog in a pack is the most powerful. He has won his position by fighting for it and showing his superiority, which he enforces by ensuring he is the one to which the others must submit. However, Matty McNair tells of a dog who did not have to fight for the position of boss dog, due to his burly size and very intimidating manner: "He just looked around the team and gave them the evil eye," she says, "communicating clearly that if any of the team challenged him, he would kill them."

In P.C. Sutherland's 1852 *Journal of a Voyage in Baffin's Bay and Barrow Straits in the Years 1850-1851*, he notes that "young dogs have a distinct understanding among themselves as to rank and prowess. If the true and understood position of an individual became disputable in the least degree, it behoved to be settled by a keen engagement, which frequently resulted in the infliction of serious wounds. Their teeth are so sharp that the wounds they leave are scarcely discernable from wounds inflicted by sharp-pointed iron weapons."

Robert Dovers, an Australian member of a 1951 French expedition team in the Antarctic who was responsible for the care of the teams' sled dogs, tells of an incident in which one of the dogs was viciously attacked by eight other dogs on the team. The poor dog was horribly mangled, with deep wounds several inches long where the dogs' teeth had dragged through skin and flesh. It seemed the only recourse was to shoot the dog and put him out of his misery, but the men had grown attached to the dog and decided to save him. They sewed up his gaping wounds and nursed him back to health. Only two weeks later, the wounds were sufficiently healed for the dog to take his place back in harness and pull his weight on the team. Dovers added

Inuit Dogs singing their evening song. *Photo: Debbie McAllister.*

that a man with such wounds would have been in the hospital for months, if not dead.

## Instinct

Inuit Dogs have an inborn instinct to pull. It is part of their genetic makeup. They also have a strong predatory instinct, which is how they survive when they are forced to fend for themselves. Inuit Dogs are independent, courageous, intelligent, alert and acutely aware of their environment. They are rough and tough, but can be very gentle, depending on how they were brought up. They also have an amazing memory. When they reach familiar territory, they know the way home, even in a blinding blizzard. They remember where their master has set a trap and will only stop there, not at someone else's.

Paul Crowley tells about a day trip he took with his Inuit Dogs to a boy-scout cabin on the north coast of Frobisher Bay. When he went back the year after, he was not able to find the trail he had previously taken, but his lead dog, Lilly the First, led him to the cabin without hesitation, even though the melting sea ice had obliterated last year's scent.

Stopping for tea.
*Photo: Debbie McAllister.*

"The dogs taught us about our land," explains Peter Andaluk, an Inuk elder who was interviewed in the documentary film "Qimmit." "They knew the land so well they would find the precise spot where we had stopped for tea the year before."

Inuit Dogs are known to be the eyes and ears of the driver. They instinctively avoid unsafe areas such as thin ice or crevasses that could endanger them by balking or refusing to move forward. Inuit elders tell of lead dogs disobeying their commands when they sense danger, thereby saving their owners' lives.

An example of the Inuit Dog's instinct to avoid danger happened during the 2008 Qimualaniq Quest, a 200-mile (320-kilometer) dog-sledding race between Iqaluit and Kimmirut on Baffin Island. One of the rangers scouting the trails on his snowmobile accidentally drove off a cliff due to poor visibility. He was found two days later, seriously injured but alive.

Siu-Ling, one of the race participants, almost went off a similar cliff that same day, but the dogs recognized danger, stopped and refused to continue, preventing an accident that could have seriously injured her. Standing on the edge of a 20-foot drop, it was impossible for her to see the terrain. It was only when she tossed stones ahead of the dogs that the steep drop became evident, forcing her to work with the dogs to find an alternate route. It is this kind of connection and understanding between the dog driver and her team that has saved many a life.

Like wolves, Inuit Dogs have what dog historian Mark Derr describes as "extra-sensory perception." Their super senses allow them to identify the moods of humans and prey, to locate someone at a distance, and to anticipate the arrival of their master. In a 2003 paper, Professor Wolfgang M. Schleidt, a specialist in animal behavior at the University of Vienna, explains that dogs, like wolves, are very much aware of "who is who, who is where, and who is doing what." Dogs pick up their master's mood and feelings. Harry Okpik, a champion dog driver from Quaqtaq, Nunavik, says, "When I am happy, the dogs are happy, and when I am sad, they are very calm, very gentle."

Shari Fox Gearheard, who lived in the Arctic for 15 years, has her own team of Inuit Dogs. She worked with Inuit hunters and elders for her research, documenting Inuit knowledge. She shares some amazing things she discovered about the spiritual and cultural side of human-dog relationships in Inuit culture and learned about the dogs' special senses and abilities that are taken very seriously by elders.

Based on stories Fox Gearheard has heard, documented and experienced with her own dogs, she has no doubt it is true. One of the abilities that she heard about was how dogs can take sickness or death away from people, as in this story from an Inuk friend who grew up and lived in an igloo with her parents:

Their only means of transportation was her father's dog team. When this friend was a baby, she fell ill with a severe chest infection. She had a high fever, was wheezing and had difficulty breathing. Her parents were quite concerned and decided to take her to a nearby settlement to seek medical care. Her father went outside to hook up the dogs while her mother stayed in the igloo with the baby, rubbing and patting her back to help her breathe.

When her father approached the dogs that were tied outside, they were eerily quiet and did not move. This was very strange, as they normally would get up and start howling and jumping in excitement when they saw him coming. He walked from dog to dog to check on them. Each just laid there quietly. When he reached his lead dog, he discovered the dog was dead.

The moment he discovered the dead dog, he heard laughter from inside the igloo. He quickly turned around and dashed inside to see his wife sitting on the sleeping platform in the igloo with a big smile on her face and the baby sitting up on her lap. She told him how the baby suddenly seemed better. It was a startling surprise. The baby girl who was so ill had made a sudden, unexpected recovery the moment the father found

CANADIAN INUIT DOG

his dead lead dog. There was no reason for the dog to have died. The family believed that their lead dog averted the baby's demise by dying in her place.

Fox Gearheard has heard other stories about Inuit Dogs that know when people are sick, and who take the sickness away.

"Having dogs for a long time now, I truly believe that they have special abilities ... and they have understanding beyond our own comprehension," Fox Gearheard says. "They have their own language, their own souls, their own way of being in the world and a special connection to the spiritual world that often people cannot see (or have long ago forgotten how to see). I feel so grateful I get to experience a little part of that. It is another wonderful aspect of these dogs."

Whether or not skeptics believe those stories, they are nonetheless a powerful example of how pivotal these dogs were in Inuit culture, not just as utilitarian helpers, but as transformative figures, helping them bridge the gap between their survival in a harsh landscape, and whatever unseen worlds might await beyond.

Inuit Dog waiting near its sled on the pack ice on Frobisher Bay, Iqaluit, Nunavut. *Photo: Carolyne Pehora.*

# Physiology

How do dogs and wolves living in the Arctic survive when temperatures drop below freezing?

The answer is endothermic thermoregulation, which produces considerable metabolic heat — the body's ability to maintain its core internal temperature, regardless of changes in the environment. In both sled dogs and wolves, the insulative properties of their thick, double-layered coat traps warm air to insulate the body and maintain heat. The insulating effectiveness of their fur is also increased through piloerection — the involuntary erection or bristling of hairs due to a sympathetic reflex that is usually triggered by cold or fear.

Like all mammals, the Inuit Dog is endothermic, or warm blooded — able to maintain a relatively constant body temperature through its metabolism in spite of widely ranging environmental temperatures. However, to stay healthy, mammals also need to keep their body temperature within a narrow range. In an Arctic climate, the challenge is that if heat loss is greater than metabolic heat production, the mammal can die. This is in contrast with some ectothermic, or coldblooded vertebrates like frogs, which can freeze solid in winter, and come "back to life" in the spring.

According to Arnold Schytte Blix, a Norwegian zoologist and professor at the University of Tromsø, heat loss from an animal can be attributed to "conduction, convection, radiation and evaporation."

Conduction is the movement or transfer of heat between two solid objects, in this case between the animal's body and the cold ground it sits or sleeps on. This heat loss can be accelerated by convection — the transfer of heat between the animal and air through movement — which, in most cases, is the wind. According to Blix, wind causes "turbulence and breaks down the insulating layer of stagnant air between the hairs of the fur." Heat loss can also be exacerbated by long-wave (infrared) radiation and evaporation from the animal's body, a process when a liquid substance becomes a gas, which depends on the difference in the temperature of body surface and the environment.

Respiration also results in additional thermal losses. Blix explains that when warm-blooded animals in an Arctic environment breathe, cold air is inhaled into the lungs, where it is warmed to body-core temperature. When the mammal exhales, warm

Huddling for warmth. *Photo: Debbie McAllister.*

air and moisture are lost, which Blix explains may represent a significant energy loss for the animal. In the Arctic, this loss of water has to be replenished either by the intake of cold water, which must be heated to body temperature, or snow, which first must be melted, resulting in an additional loss of energy.

Some mammals use hibernation to survive Arctic winters, which involves reducing movement and lowering their body temperature. Dogs don't hibernate. However, when resting, to minimize heat loss Inuit Dogs create a shallow indentation in the snow before lying down. They curl into a ball to reduce body surface exposed to the cold, and cover their faces with their bushy tail to warm the air they breathe. In a snowstorm, they let themselves be snowed down. The snow acts as insulation. Once a storm has passed, they shake off their snowy cloak and are ready to get back to work. On a sunny day, solar radiation and huddling contribute to the warming of the animal.

The body temperature of Inuit Dogs and wolves is between 101.3° and 103° Fahrenheit (38.5° to 39.6° Celsius). It is warmer than the temperature in their legs, which aren't as well insulated as their bodies. To prevent heat loss from their legs and keep their limbs from freezing, Arctic mammals like Inuit Dogs, Arctic wolves, deer, foxes and musk oxen have a system of special blood vessels that restrict heat loss from their legs and feet. Called a counter-current heat exchange, this complex network of blood vessels to the extremities keeps them from suffering frost damage. The deep arteries and veins in the legs are closely aligned, so that cooled venous blood (blood returning to the heart) in the legs picks up heat from warm arterial blood (blood coming from the heart). In this way, warm arterial blood re-warms venous blood flowing through limbs that have been chilled by the cold. By the time venous blood from the legs reaches the heart, it is not as cold and so minimizes heart strain.

These hardy animals also have a protective mechanism that prevents their footpads from freezing on cold surfaces like snow and ice. Wildlife veterinarian Terry Kreeger explains that special unbranched arteries carry blood directly through the footpad to a complex network of nerves and blood vessels located in the paw and toe pads. Because this heat exchange is located in the pad surface that touches the cold ground, Inuit dogs are able to withstand the cold surfaces they stand on. Heat flow to the feet is minimized, resulting in a low foot temperature and reduced heat loss to the environment. This keeps the foot temperature of Arctic dogs such as the Inuit Dog just above the tissue-freezing point around 32° F (0° C) when they are at rest in sub-zero temperatures.

# Diet

Inuit Dogs eat whatever the human hunter catches and shares with them: seal, whale, walrus, fish or caribou. Inuit Dogs can devour up to five pounds of meat in a single meal, but they can also go without food for days and still pull a *qamutiik*. Inuit Dogs not only eat the meat of their prey, they also eat the hair, feathers, skin, bones and organs, which are sources of vitamins, protein, calcium, fat and minerals. When they are working in cold weather, they need a lot of calories.

In "Sled Dog Science," a 2009 article in *Scientific American*, Krista West writes that "sled dogs seem to flip an inner switch that acutely changes how they burn fat calories, allowing them to keep going and going and going with no obvious pain."

Like wolves, Inuit Dogs still behave like predators. When forced to fend for themselves, they catch and kill rodents, birds, hares, and sometimes caribou and young polar bears. Nowadays, dogs kept in a dog yard are also fed a high-protein and high-fat commercial kibble that should not contain any grain products. Paul Crowley says Inuit Dogs like *igunaq* — fermented walrus. It is supposed to be better for them than fresh meat.

Cutting up seal meat to feed the dogs. *Photo source: Siu-Ling Han.*

In a 2005 study, Linn Anne Brunborg, a nutritionist and health manager at Orka Foods Norway, and her team analyzed the nutritional composition of blubber and the meat of hooded seal (*Cystophora cristata*) and harp seal (*Phagophilus groenlandicus*) from Greenland. They found that "seal blubber is an excellent source of long and very long chain (VLC) n-3 polyunsaturated fatty acids (PUFAs), in addition to long and VLC monounsaturated fatty acids (MUFAs)." Seal meat is one of the best marine foods. It is an excellent source of vitamins A, B12 and D3, as well as iron, zinc and selenium. Working dogs fed seal meat, blubber and skin in winter have better endurance

Inuit Dog wolfing down a chunk of seal meat. *Photo: Shari Fox Gearheard.*

and are better able to maintain body temperature than dogs fed on caribou, fish or kibble. Zinc is needed to fight infection and promote the healing of wounds. Iron is required for healthy blood and energy, and selenium is an antioxidant that prevents cells in the body from damage.

Most sled dogs don't drink water in winter, although they do gulp down snow, even though snow does not contain much water. While four or five inches of heavy, wet snow can contain one inch of water, it may take 20 inches of dry powdery snow to equal one inch of water.

So, how do sled dogs get hydrated? According to Dr. Jerry Vanek, a musher and sled-dog-race veterinarian, "the most successful sled dogs carry their water on the inside." He explains that a sled dog's body is 70 percent water: "No water, no dog." One of the most important sources of water for a sled dog is in the food it eats — what Vanek calls "pre-formed water." For humans, pre-formed water is found in watermelons and strawberries, which contain 92 percent water, followed by grapefruit, cantaloupe and peaches. High-water-content vegetables are cucumber, lettuce, zucchini, radish and celery. For sled dogs, chunks of moist, frozen meat and fish are full of water. Seal meat with blubber contains 45 percent water, 18 percent protein and 39 percent fat, whereas lean seal meat contains 72 percent water, 27 percent protein and less than 1 percent fat.

In winter, 80 percent of a sled dog's water consumption comes in a "pre-formed manner." They don't drink it, but rather eat it. "When fats in the diet are broken down for energy, oxygen is combined with the carbons and hydrogens of the fatty acids to make carbon dioxide which is exhaled, and water — some of which is retained by the body," Vanek explains. "In other words, a portion of the water the dog drinks is actually the result of a chemical reaction in the dog's body as it burns up food for energy."

The Canadian Inuit Dog is a wonder of nature. His remarkable physiology and ability to withstand the harsh rigors of the Arctic, and the unique bond he has with his human family, made him survive in one of the most unforgiving environments on earth for thousands of years. It is up to us to keep and preserve this wonder of nature into the future.

# 5

# Pack Structure

A definite hierarchy ensures that Inuit sled dogs all know their place and work together

Like wolves, Inuit Dogs have a strong sense of pack dynamics and social order, and a hierarchy with an *angajuqqaaqtaq* (alpha dog) at the head of the pack. In Inuit Dog society, the *angajuqqaaqtaq* is the boss dog. He is the strongest, most dominant and most intimidating male.

He rules over the other dogs in the pack. At feeding time, the boss dog is always the first to eat. Inuit Dog expert Ken MacRury says boss dogs are "born with a certain mental attitude." A puppy that is observed to always win a fight, is not afraid or shy, and is the one who always eats first, is a good candidate for boss dog, especially if he is alert and always asserts himself.

A good boss dog does not look for trouble. He is the one in control. He asserts his superiority by staring and growling to keep order in the pack. The boss dog is usually assisted by a male sibling who acts as "lieutenant." The lieutenant helps the boss dog mete out discipline and break up fights among the other dogs. Dogs of lower rank are expected to show respect for the boss dog when he approaches by licking his muzzle and rolling on their backs .

In a 2003 interview with *The Fan Hitch*, MacRury explains that "a good boss dog is critical to a well-ordered team, for without one, the team will verge on anarchy all the time. When you have a good boss dog, there will be calm order in the team, as the boss will not allow others to fight and will not start fights himself."

MacRury notes that an important part of a boss dog's development is the opportunity to interact with his pack without human interference. "If we are forever rushing in to break up every squabble, it does not allow the natural boss to emerge, or the team social structure to develop."

Boss dog (foreground) after a fight. *Photo: Debbie McAllister.*

The boss dog's demeanor is one of quiet confidence, backed up by decisive action if he is unduly provoked. Sometimes there is a fight for power but, eventually, the loser either accepts the other dog's dominance , or gets killed. Some Inuit Dog owners who care for the boss dog and become aware of the old dog's waning supremacy will mercifully pull him from the team to be retired, to keep him from getting killed.

When Toko, a retired boss dog we adopted, encountered a scrappy little terrier on a walk, he just stopped and glared at the frantically barking, snarling critter. He continued to stare, as the plucky little dog edged closer. When the terrier invaded his space, the former boss dog suddenly grabbed it by the scruff of its neck and shook it a couple of times before dropping it, as if to say: "There you go! You'd better show some respect!" And with that he walked away, his dignity intact.-

A lieutenant standing atop a dog house that he never sleeps in. *Photo: Kim Han.*

## Behavior

MacRury says that behavior is a complex mechanism determined by a combination of instinct, genetics, evolution and selective breeding. Dogs are social animals, and their special bond with humans goes back thousands of years.

Some scientists see the dog as a wolf that never grew into adulthood, because its characteristics are very similar to those of juvenile wolves. Physical examples are the smaller head of the dog, its shorter muzzle, steeper forehead and more crowded teeth. These paedomorphic features, or neoteny, is when adults retain traits seen only in juveniles. The submissive behavior of wolf cubs toward adult wolves can also be seen in the way an

Rolling over on the back and exposing the belly is a universal canine sign of submission. *Photo: Siu-Ling Han.*

adult dog shows its submissiveness toward its human master, for instance, by crouching, licking and rolling on its back.

In an interview with *The Fan Hitch*, MacRury explained that selection of pups for his team depended on their behavioral traits. Pups have to prove that they are "willing workers able to go the distance. They must above all be part of the team, even though they are at the bottom of the hierarchy, deferential to the older adults, no fighting, and they must learn quickly to respond to the driver's commands, when to go, when to stop, lie down,

Conflicts over hierarchy within the pack can sometimes escalate to the point of death. *Photo: Siu-Ling Han.*

stay in tight with the team, etc." In other words, they have to listen well, be obedient, and be eager to work hard and keep up with the team.

## Temperament and Socialization

The biggest difference between an Inuit Dog and a wolf is that the Inuit Dog is domesticated and the wolf is not. The Inuit Dog has very strong predatory instincts and, therefore, makes a good hunting assistant. In summer, when the dogs are not working, some owners take their dogs to an island where they have to fend for themselves and forage for their own food, catching

Puppies and children are a natural combination. *Photo courtesy Allen Gordon.*

mice, lemmings, birds, fish or whatever they can find.

"Predatory aggressive behavior was not only a result of their partnership with a hunting society in the acquisition of animals as food and other raw materials," explains Sue Hamilton in her 2011 paper *Defining the Inuit Dog*, "but also for their own survival when not being fed directly by humans."

A retired Inuit Dog that was taken for an off-leash walk in a wooded area, south of the treeline, was found in a clearing, munching on a squirrel he had just caught. All his master could see was the dog's happy face as he wolfed down the squirrel, and how the squirrel's tail quickly became shorter and shorter, as it disappeared down the dog's gullet. In the Arctic, Inuit Dogs have been seen catching birds in flight.

Inuit Dog pups should be socialized as early as possible, and treated with respect and a firm hand, preferably from birth. Human contact at this stage of a puppy's life is essential if it is to become a well-behaved working animal that listens to its master. Puppies born in *ilagiit nunagivaktangat* (camps) were raised by women and children.

Generally, Inuit Dogs are very friendly, although some tend to be aloof with outsiders. While most of them adapt well to strangers or dogs they are not familiar with, caution is advised, especially, with regards to small children and small, yappy dogs. They should never be left alone with these dogs, especially, when they start whimpering or running.

Inuit Dogs are sociable within their own pack – as long as they are not fighting for dominance. As they become seniors , well-trained Inuit Dogs are inclined to mellow with age. Based

This retired boss dog and former lead dog became an affectionate house dog in retirement. *Photo: Siu-Ling Han.*

Eskimo children with puppies. Moravian Mission Station, Bethel, Alaska, 1900-1930. *Source: Library of Congress.*

on my personal experience, they become more affectionate. Retired Inuit Dogs that were well raised still have a lot to give. It is, however, of the utmost importance for people thinking of adopting a retired Inuit Dog to familiarize themselves with this kind of dog. They must know how to handle him and ensure the dog knows who the alpha is. A well-behaved retired Inuit Dog is a joy to have around, especially, when he starts communicating with you, with gentle howls as he nudges you and shows you how much he loves you.

## Inuit Traditional Knowledge

Because dogs played such an important role in Inuit life, the skills involved in raising a good dog team, knowing how to handle the dogs and taking care of them were part of Inuit *qaujimajatuqangit* (IQ), or Inuit traditional knowledge.

In her 2010 master's thesis, Kerrie Ann Shannon describes the importance of understanding an Inuit Dog's behavior. It was used, for example, to predict certain weather conditions, such as the onset or end of a storm.

One Inuit Elder explained that his dogs would warn of an approaching storm when they started shaking themselves on a clear day. That gave people a chance to be prepared before a storm arrived. When dogs started jumping around with excitement during a storm, it was a sign that the weather was about to clear. The knowledge gained from understanding the dogs, their behavior, and how they interact with other dogs on the team help determine a dog's function on the team – for instance, if he or she would make a good lead dog. A good lead dog is eager to please. He, or she, is confident to go ahead

### WHAT'S IN A NAME?

Inuit have different names for their dogs. Dogs on dog teams are *qimmuksit*. (Singular is *qimmuksiq*.) It distinguishes them from dogs that do not pull sleds. *Qimmimarik* means "pure dog," the traditional dog of their ancestors. Plural is *Qimmimariit*. The term is used to distinguish them from mixed breeds and dogs brought up north by *qallunaat*. *Qimmitsiaq* is "a good dog." Plural is *qimmitsiat*, and *qimmituinnaq* is just an ordinary dog: not a leader or boss dog.

of other dogs and has to be a dog that other dogs will follow. According to MacRury, lead dogs are usually female.

In her 2010 book *The Empire of Ice: Encounters in a Changing Landscape*, Gretel Ehrlich relates a story about an Inuk going on a walrus hunt that turned dangerous because of moving ice. The hunter took an old, retired dog with him and put him on the shortest trace so he hardly had to pull. Inuit Dogs are supremely aware of their surroundings, and the old dog knew which way the ice was moving and when to get off before it broke away. The dog knew which way to go because he could feel the currents and direction of the wind. That is why it was important for the dog driver to understand his dogs' behavior, body language, and intentions to keep him and his team safe.

This kind of knowledge was shared and passed down from one generation to the next, the way Elijah's father passed his knowledge about the skillful handling and managing of dogs on to his son. It was part of growing up.

After 11 puppies, this Inuit Dog mother takes a well-deserved rest. *Photo: Siu-Ling Han.*

# Reproduction

The alpha dog in a team will breed with any female in heat. Female dogs come into estrus twice a year — though not tied to any particular season or time of year — and therefore are able to have two litters a year, although it is rare if the first litter earlier that year survives. Female wolves come into estrus only once in early winter, usually between late January and early April.

Wolf pups are born in early spring, which allows them to grow during the warm season in order to survive winter. In dogs, gestation is approximately 63 days. Inuit Dog puppies born in spring and summer are better able to survive the winter those born in autumn or winter. Pups that survive the winter are strong — a matter of survival of the fittest. Pups that do not thrive at

Inuit Dogs should be handled from birth to continually strengthen the human-animal bond. *Photo: Siu-Ling Han.*

birth are usually destroyed. Sometimes, the mother buries them in the snow, or carries them away and leaves them to die.

A litter can be as small as one and as large as ten, sometimes more. Since today's Inuit Dogs are domesticated, people breeding them keep them in outdoor sheds, garages or snow houses, where newborn puppies are protected from the elements. It is not unusual for an owner to stay with the bitch as she is whelping. It gives the owner a chance to handle the pups as soon as they are born, to create a bond between human and dog. This involves a lot of trust on the part of the dam.

Dogs and wolves share the same genes, which means they could interbreed and produce fertile young, but Jennifer Leonard, an evolutionary biologist at the Smithsonian's Institute of Natural History, has found no evidence that dogs in the New World ever bred with wolves. Assertions of interbreeding between the species are "unreliable and unsubstantiated," MacRury agrees in his thesis, noting that there is no real proof of interbreeding between wolves and dogs. One factor against this unlikely liaison is that Inuit Dogs have an instinctive fear of wolves. Wolves consider Inuit Dogs prey and will kill and eat any Inuit Dog if they have the chance. Numerous Inuit Dogs that were chained in isolated areas in the Northwest Territories and Nunavik have been killed by wolves. MacRury tells of a number of instances where Inuit Dogs were attacked by wolves in outpost camps outside Igloolik, Clyde and Iqaluit in Nunavut. Sometimes the dogs were killed and dragged away to be eaten, and sometimes the wolves were driven off by the combined team and/or team owner. MacRury also tells of a case where a team of Inuit Dogs at a camp outside Igloolik actually ganged up on a lone wolf and killed it. In a December 2005 article in *The Fan Hitch*, Allen Gordon of Kuujjuaq, Nunavik, tells how a wolf had "made a meal out of a puppy," and how wolves had killed pet dogs and sled-dog puppies that were picketed just outside Kuujjuaq.

Another reason it is doubtful that dogs and wolves in Canada interbred is that male wolves are fertile only once a year. Opportunities for a male wolf to breed with a female dog are rare, as the female dog would have to be in estrus during the brief period the male wolf was fertile in order to conceive.

Wolves that domesticated themselves thousands of years ago by following humans evolved into dogs and became part of the human family. As such, they live with humans, share in their lives, assist in the hunt for food, protect their humans and, in turn, are taken care of by humans, which often include feeding, breeding and assisting when bitches whelp.

# 6

# Contributions to Arctic Life

From hunting companion to intrepid explorer

To Inuit, dogs were more than just a means to carry packs, pull heavily loaded sleds and convey people from place to place. They also were hunting assistants, companions and protectors.

In death as in life, the Inuit Dog proved its value. In times of famine it could be a source of food, but Inuit would only consume their dogs in extreme circumstances when there was absolutely nothing to eat. When a dog dies, its skin can be used to make clothing, and its fur to make *kamikpait*, the socks worn between the inner socks and the *kamik* (boot). Inuit use *qimmiq* skin to make mitts because it does not freeze and is very warm.

*Preceding page: Inuit Dogs in harness. Photo: Looqi Schmidt.*

*An Inuit family from Inukjuak wearing traditional boot, or kamik. Photo: Heiko Wittenborn/ Nunavik Tourism.*

Ken MacRury had a pair of dog-skin mitts and *kamikpait*, as well as a pair of dog-skin pants. "It takes three dogs to make a pair of pants," he says. "They were incredibly warm, could be worn only when the temperature was lower than -30 degrees. The mitts were so warm that I personally could not wear them, although I carried them with me for years and loaned them to others who had cold hands." *Qimmiq* fur was also used to trim the hoods of parkas to protect the face from the wind.

Because of their nature-honed instincts and tenacity, Inuit Dogs contributed, directly and indirectly, not only to daily life, but to Inuit survival and the very history of this inhospitable region, helping in efforts to map its geography, and document natural and cultural life.

Archival photo of Inuit hunters with sled dogs at an *aglu*. Photo: Richard Harrington. *Courtesy: Library and Archives Canada.*

## Hunting

There is an Inuit saying that a hunter without dogs is only half a hunter. As partners in their hunt for food, the dogs of Inuit made a difference between survival and extinction in a harsh polar environment where food was scarce and people could not rely on plants for their subsistence.

When hunting on sea ice with his master, the Inuit Dog's superior sense of smell is essential for finding seal breathing holes in the ice known as *agluit* (plural for *aglu*). An *aglu* is an opening in the surface of sea ice made by a seal. It is difficult for hunters to find, because it looks like a slightly protruding snow-covered mound on the uneven surface of the frozen sea.

Once the dog has led a hunter to an *aglu*, the hunter patiently waits for the seal to return to breathe, so he can capture it with his harpoon. He sometimes has to stand at the *aglu* for hours and keep very still for a seal to appear. Seal is one of the

*From left: Caribou, musk oxen and polar bears. Photos: Dreamstime.*

most valuable food sources for Inuit and their dogs. It contains omega-3, fat, vitamins and minerals. Inuit elder Jeannie Padluq, Elijah's wife, says eating seal meat warms the body.

Elijah was between seven and eight years old when he went on his first hunting trip with his father. He remembers hunting for walrus, ringed seals and bearded seals at the floe edge. He discovered how to find seal holes, and had a lot of fun learning as he went along. Inuit dogs were not only used to find an *aglu* to catch seal, but also to help with the tracking down and hunting of polar bears and musk oxen, and to hold them at bay for the hunter to make his kill. The dogs were also used to run down wounded caribou, knock them down, and keep them there until the hunter could arrive.

According to Elijah, dogs can smell when a polar bear is near, even if people don't see it. The dogs prick their ears forward and start running at an increased pace, even though the bear would

*From left: Bearded seal, walrus and ring seal. Photos: Ondrej Prosicky, Vladimir Seliverstoff and Anthony Hathaway.*

CANADIAN INUIT DOG

be more than half a mile (one kilometer) away. "The dogs would get really excited," Elijah remembers. "Their barking is not the same as a normal barking sound. It's a different sound." He says dogs prevent the polar bear from getting too close to people, but keep it from running away by surrounding it, barking, growling and biting its ankles, where the bear cannot reach them. When the bear is too exhausted to run away, the hunter either harpoons or shoots it.

For thousands of years, humans' existence in the Canadian Arctic was closely linked to their dogs. Care and management of a dog team was an integral part of Inuit culture, daily life and survival. The Qikiqtani Truth Commission (QTC) Final Report in 2013 explains that the closeness of the relationship between an Inuk hunter and his dogs is captured in the Inuktitut term for dog team: *qimuksiq*, which includes both the *qimmit* (plural for dog) and the *qimmusiktiq* (dog driver), as they travel from one *ilagiit nunagivaktangat* (camp) to another.

In summer, dogs carried packs. In winter, they served as draught animals, pulling hunters and their equipment for hunting trips, and to visit trap lines. After the hunt, the dogs pulled sleds loaded with the hunters' catch back to camp or trading posts.

Nowadays most Inuit travel by snowmobile, although dog sled is still considered safer, especially in a blizzard, when visibility can be near zero. White-out conditions also impede a sense of distance and direction due to heavy cloud cover and flat light conditions, when there are no shadows in a nearly featureless, snow-covered landscape that has no horizon.

## Polar Exploration

Not surprisingly, Inuit Dogs were in harness when explorers of various eras set off to traverse northernmost North America, from the Atlantic to Pacific coasts.

The unsung heroes of polar history, these hardy, hard-working dogs who accompanied and supported explorers and scientists to the North and South poles before the invention of snowmobiles were not always treated with care. Many suffered abuse and starvation, and paid for it with the ultimate sacrifice

The Gjøa, the first vessel to transit the Northwest Passage in 1906 with Roald Amundsen. *Photo: Dreamstime.*

Bust of polar explorer Roald Amundsen in front of the Polar Museum in Tromso, Norway. *Photo: Dmitry Chulov.*

in humankind's quest for survival, honor, fame and fortune. Without these dogs, 19th and early 20th Century polar explorers would not have conquered the Arctic.

Norwegian explorer Captain Roald Amundsen (1872-1928), also known as "The Last Viking," was the first to navigate the entire Northwest Passage from the Atlantic to the Pacific Ocean. In June 1903, Amundsen set sail from Oslo on the Gjøa, a fishing boat he prepared for the expedition. During a two-year stay in a small sheltered bay on King William Island north of the Canadian mainland now known as Gjøa Haven, Amundsen made friends with local Inuit, the Netsilik, from whom he learned Arctic survival skills and how to travel across ice by dog team. His east-west journey ended at Herschel Island in the Yukon when his ship became trapped in sea ice, where it remained all winter.

Anxious to tell the world about the expedition's success, Amundsen traveled almost 500 miles (800 kilometers) by dog sled to Eagle City, Alaska, to send telegraphs about the success of his expedition to the outside world. He later joined his crew on the Gjøa, and on August 25, 1906, Amundsen traversed the Northwest Passage, a seaway across the Arctic linking the Atlantic and Pacific Oceans, through the Canadian Arctic Archipelago, into the Beaufort Sea and into the Pacific Ocean through the Chukchi and Bering Sea.

Amundsen was also the first explorer to reach the South Pole with four companions, a carefully selected team of 52 sled dogs and four sledges. He started from the Bay of Whales on Antarctica's Ross Shelf on October 19, 1911, reaching the South Pole on December 14, 1911. After spending six weeks at the Pole, Amundsen and his crew returned to base camp on January 25, 1912. The voyage took 99 days and 1,860 miles (2994 kilometers). Amundsen referred to his dogs as "our children" and stated "dogs are the most important thing for us. The whole outcome of the expedition depends on them."

Amundsen's favorite dogs, Fix and Lassesin, resting during his 1911 Antarctic expedition. *Source: U.S. Library of Congress.*

In 1909, Commander Robert Peary (1856-1920) used dog teams in his quest to reach the North Pole. In his book *The North Pole.*

*Its Discovery in 1909 under Auspices of the Peary Arctic Club*, Peary writes: "Before taking up the story of our advance from Cape York, a word ought to be said about those remarkable creatures, the Eskimo dogs, for without their help success could never have crowned the efforts of the expedition. They are sturdy, magnificent animals. There may

Robert Peary, 1909 self-portrait.

be larger dogs than these, there may be handsomer dogs; but I doubt it. Other dogs may work as well or travel as fast and far when fully fed; but there is no dog in the world that can work so long in the lowest temperatures on practically nothing to eat."

Peary was right: These hard-working dogs are known to be able to survive without food for weeks. In her 1977 book *The World of Sled Dogs*, biologist and sled dog racer Lorna Coppinger writes, "It is a common experience, while traveling, for dogs to go for several days destitute of food with no visible diminution of strength or spirits. This, of course, is never required of them except under stress of unavoidable circumstances."

Polar explorer and anthropologist Knud Rasmussen (1879-1933), the son of a Danish missionary and Danish-Inuit mother, was the first European to travel the entire Northwest Passage across Canada and Alaska by dog sled. Rasmussen and a friend, Peter Freuchen, established a Thule Trading Station at Cape York (Uummannaq) in Greenland, the most northerly trading post in the world, which became the home base for Rasmussen's Thule

Expeditions between 1912 and 1933.

On his first expedition in April 1912, Rasmussen and Freuchen sought to verify Robert Peary's claim that a channel divided

Peary Land from Greenland. They selected two experienced Inuit hunters to join them on their expedition: an Inuk named Uvdloriaq, who was known as a superior hunter, and Inukitsoq, who had been on two polar expeditions with Peary. They traveled more than 600 miles (1,000 kilometers) across the intimidating Greenland Ice Cap, starting in Thule, on Greenland's northwest coast, north to the Clements Markham Glacier, then east toward Independence Fjord in northeast Greenland.

Knud Rasmussen.

Rasmussen and Freuchen were able to prove that Peary was wrong: Peary Land was part of Greenland and not a separate island. Stephen Bown, author of *White Eskimo*, a biography about Knud Rasmussen, wrote that Rasmussen and his team started this journey with 53 dogs. They came back with only eight, as many dogs had perished during this gruelling journey that almost cost the men their lives. Clements Markham, then president of the Royal Geographic Society, called the journey "the finest ever performed by dogs."

It was, however, the fifth Thule Expedition, from 1921 to 1924, that was considered Rasmussen's greatest achievement. Rasmussen and a team of seven left the shores of Greenland for Arctic Canada by ship on September 7, 1921, arriving 11 days later in the bay of a small island they later named Danish Island, where they established a base camp. From there they traveled by dog teams, covering the entire eastern Arctic, particularly the areas around Igloolik, Pond Inlet and Chesterfied, where they collected geological and botanical specimens and conducted interviews and archaeological excavations, before Rasmussen left with two Greenlanders by dog sled to Nome, Alaska. They traveled a distance of 3,728 miles (6,000 kilometers) in 15 months, completing their sledge journey at Icy Cape, Alaska, on June 8, 1924.

In 1968, iconic polar explorer Wally Herbert led the British Trans-Arctic Expedition (BTAE) on a 16-month journey from Point Barrow, Alaska, to the North Pole, via the Point of Inaccessibility, to Spitsbergen. Herbert was accompanied by Allan Gill, Fritz Koerner and Ken Hedges. They traveled a distance of 3,620 miles (5,826 kilometers) with 40 Inuit Dogs. It was the first surface crossing of the Arctic Ocean with dog teams, and the second confirmed expedition to reach the North Pole. Harold Wilson, then British prime minister, hailed it as "a feat of endurance and courage ..."

Naomi Uemura, a Japanese explorer and mountaineer, did a solo sled-dog run from Thule, Greenland, to Kotzebue, Alaska, with a team of Inuit Dogs. Uemura travelled through Canada's Arctic over two winters between 1974 and 1976, in 363 days. He set an extraordinary long-distance record of 7,452 miles (12,000 kilometers), in preparation for his solo North Pole trip in 1978. Although some sources state that Uemura was traveling with Alaskan Malamutes, Bill Carpenter, who met Uemura, insists Uemura's dogs were Inuit Dogs from Greenland and Canada. On March 7, 1978, Uemura travelled 478 miles (770 kilometers) with a team of dogs from Cape Edward, Ellesmere Island, to the North Pole.

In 1968, iconic polar explorer Wally Herbert led the British Trans-Atlantic Expedition on a 16-month journey from Point Barrow, Alaska, to the North Pole, via the Point of Inaccessibility, to Spitsbergen. *Painting by Wally Herbert.* © Herbert Collection, Polarworld, www.polarworld.co.uk.

# Scientific Discovery

On June 24, 1893, Norwegian explorer Fridtjof Nansen (1861-1930) left the port of Kristiania with a crew of 12 men and provisions for four years, headed for the New Siberian Islands, an archipelago located in the Arctic Ocean between the Laptev Sea and East Siberian Sea.

Nansen wanted to find out if he would be able to reach the Pole, or as close to the Pole as possible, by boat, on the strong east-west ocean currents over the polar sea along the northern Siberian coast toward Greenland. Drifting along on the Fram, a vessel especially built to withstand being squashed by sea ice and fast-shifting ice floes, they made very slow progress and moved only a few miles a day. After the Fram became stuck in sea ice in September 1893, Nansen decided to leave the Fram on March 14, 1895, and reach the pole by land.

In a January 2009 article in *National Geographic*, American historian Hampton Sides tells how Nansen and Hjalmar Johansen, a "dog-driving expert and army lieutenant, attempted to reach the Pole on skis," accompanied by 28 dogs, dragging three

Equipment belonging to polar explorers Nansen and Amundsen. *Photo: Dreamstime.*

loaded sleds and two kayaks to cross over open water with them." Sides described their journey as a "desperate journey [which] must surely rank as one of the most miserable and arduous polar slogs ever attempted." When they started running out of food, they killed off their dogs one by one to feed the remaining ones, by "cutting their throats to save on ammunition." A harsh reality!

By the time Nansen and Johansen finally arrived back in Norway in August 1896, they did not have a single dog left. Those noble animals were used and sacrificed in an attempt to reach the pole. Nansen and Johansen didn't quite make it there, but went as far north as anyone had ever been at the time. They arrived back in Norway to a hero's welcome. Nansen later became known as "a pioneer of polar exploration" and "one of the greatest men Norway has ever nurtured." Nothing was said of any of the dogs and their ultimate sacrifice.

Otto Sverdrup (1854-1930), one of Norway's foremost explorers, accompanied Nansen across Greenland in 1888, and on Nansen's polar expedition between 1893 and 1896. Sverdrup led the second Norwegian Arctic Expedition between 1898 and 1902 to the Arctic Archipelago, a group of islands in the High Arctic, north of the Canadian mainland. He traveled by dog sled to conduct extensive scientific investigations in meteorology, botany, zoology, geology, palaeontology, mineralogy and terrestrial magnetism. He also made valuable topographical observations, explored and charted Ellesmere Island, and discovered Axel Heiberg Island, Canada's second northernmost island in the Qikiqtaaluk region of Nunavut.

According to the Fram Museum website, "Sverdrup was convinced that Greenland Dogs were the best. They were friendly, strong and excellent hunting dogs ... When the dogs got the faint [sic] of polar bears or musk oxen they were nearly impossible to handle. The only way to stop the dogs then was to overturn the sledges. They soon learnt that if they wanted to go hunting, the dogs had to be released from the sledges. Five to six dogs could pull 400 kilos. Dogs and sledges were able to make progress everywhere, in all sorts of temperatures."

Almost two decades later, the British Antarctic Survey (BAS) used sled dogs from Arctic Canada, Labrador and Greenland for polar travel and scientific expeditions in Antarctica from 1945 until 1994. The dogs were more reliable than motorized vehicles over rough terrain and were not as heavy. Between 1960 and 1970, dogs were gradually replaced by snowmobiles for overland field parties. In 1994, governments responsible for scientific operations in Antarctica signed a treaty banning all non-indigenous animals on the continent, including dogs. Their overall objective was to conserve Antarctic biodiversity.

Antarctica. *Photo: Dreamstime.*

The reason why all dogs were banished from Antarctica was reported by Mark Hamilton, who attended the 2003 Marguerite Bay Reunion of the Falkland Islands Dependencies Survey/British

Antarctic Survey veterans.

"It seems that France and Argentina, for their own reasons, did not want the treaty but were unwilling to be seen as the sources of its failure," he wrote in *The Fan Hitch*. "Instead, having made the assumption that the dogs were such an integral part of British effort and traditions in Antarctica as to be something they would refuse to relinquish, the French and Argentines had the provision about the removal of non-indigenous species added to the treaty ... Their assumption was that while other countries with dogs (such as Australia and New Zealand) would be willing to give up their dogs, the provision would serve as a 'poison pill' for the BAS and result in the treaty failing because Britain would refuse to sign. Ultimately, however, word came down 'from on high' that a major treaty would not be lost over a bunch of dogs, and BAS was ordered to get rid of them."

Hamilton mentioned "the veterans' love and respect for the dogs, the bitterness of the dogs' removal from the continent, and the sense of profound loss that virtually no genetic material from this unique population was saved."

In a 1976 article in *Dogs in Canada*, biologist Bill Carpenter writes that "the Canadian Defence Research Board, during their scientific studies in the Lake Hazen area of northern Ellesmere Island from 1957 to 1959, used Eskimo dogs both for sledging and packing. One pack trip in particular covered a distance of 200 miles (320 kilometers) from Hazen Camp to Alert and back." Operation Hazen was one of the most comprehensive scientific research projects ever to be carried out in the Canadian High Arctic that focused on glaciological studies.

# Law Enforcement

More than a century ago, the North West Mounted Police (NWMP), later known as the Royal Canadian Mounted Police (RCMP), used Inuit Dogs to patrol in remote northern communities. Traveling by dog sled between 1873 and 1969, the Mounties investigated crimes and apprehended suspects. They also delivered mail, collected customs duties, established meteorological records, took the census, and provided medical aid and relief supplies. In addition, they inoculated dogs against rabies, distemper and canine hepatitis. According to the "RCMP Final Report and Review of Allegations Concerning Inuit Sled Dogs," the RCMP also provided Inuit families with RCMP sled-dog pups "when disease or starvation had partially or completely wiped out their dog team."

# Military Duty

As described earlier, the ancient migration of dogs across the North American Arctic reached all the way to Greenland. Although this book is about the Canadian Inuit Dog, one cannot overlook the contribution of the more eastern members of this aboriginal landrace that populated Greenland and ultimately served humans in a most unique way as members of the Slædepatruljen Sirius, or Sirius Dog Sled Patrol, Denmark's elite dog-sled unit.

The first dog-sled patrol, code-named Operation Resolute, was established during World War II to monitor and destroy German weather bases, and to keep Greenland in Allied hands. During the Cold War, Denmark decided to make this military presence permanent, and in 1953, the patrol became known as Sirius, after the brightest star in the dog constellation.

The Sirius Patrol is a special-force unit created under the administration of the Danish Defense Command. Its primary purpose was to conduct military surveillance and maintain national sovereignty. Headquartered in Daneborg, Northeast Greenland, the Sirius Patrol is the world's only military dog-sled operation. Six dog-sledge teams of up to a dozen dogs each, manned by two soldiers, spend up to six months traversing north and northeast Greenland between January and June, and between November and December, in an area of more than 60,000 square miles (160,000 square kilometers) for up to two years. The soldiers' training includes dog handling, winter

A Greenland Dog takes a well-deserved rest from his Sirius patrol duties. *Photo courtesy of Danish Defense Command.*

survival skills, first aid, radio and communications, firefighting and shooting, as well as cooking and sewing. Men and dogs depend on each other, as did Inuit and their dogs, keeping each other company from day to day. These men and their dogs deserve the greatest respect for their ability to work so closely together. As the human-dog relationship has been described, the presence, behavior and companionship of the dogs should not be underestimated.

Dog sledding is still considered the best way to travel long distances in Greenland. Dogs have saved their human partners' lives many times, especially when traveling at night in a fog or blizzard, once again proving the value of these remarkable dogs.

# 7

# On the Brink of Extinction

**Modern life forever changed Inuit tradition —
along with dogs' role in Arctic culture**

W hen Inuit were nomadic, most families only had between three and five dogs. But all that changed in the early 1900s, when fox fur became fashionable.

Demand led to a rapid and widespread establishment of trading posts throughout the Arctic. More Inuit became involved in trapping, traveling longer distances with their dogs to set traps on routes that sometimes stretched over a hundred or more kilometers. In summer, some dogs were dropped off on islands to fend for themselves. Others were used to travel to summer hunting grounds, carrying small paniers with food and other

*On the preceding page:* Contemplating the horizon. *Photo: Dreamstime.*

Fox stoles were the height of fashion in the Roaring Twenties. *Photo: Dreamstime.*

necessities on their backs, or put in harness to tow boats along the coast. The rest of the year, the dogs tracked and carried furs to trading posts managed by the Hudson Bay Company, which traded food and supplies to trappers, many of whom no longer had enough time to go hunting.

Inuit Dog with panier at Taloyok, formerly Spence Bay. *Photo: Richard Harrington. Courtesy Library and Archives Canada.*

With the flourishing of the fur trade, and because the Royal Canadian Mounted Police and Hudson Bay often hired locals with sleds and strong dogs to haul supplies, the number of sled dogs in Canada's Arctic increased rapidly. John McGrath, an economic-development officer with the Northwest Territories government, estimated there were around 20,000 dogs in Canada's Arctic in the 1920s, based on the number of dogs counted by settlement managers, police and the Hudson Bay Company.

The collapse of the fox fur trade in the late 1940s had a catastrophic effect on Inuit, leaving trappers without a source of income. Greenlandic explorer Knud Rasmussen lamented the "lonely Eskimo trapper" who had died of starvation while his tent "overflowed with furs."

In response, Ottawa increased its involvement in the Arctic, relocating Inuit from *ilagiit nunagivaktangit* (seasonal camps) to government-created permanent settlements, so the old and infirm could get medical treatment, and children could attend school. A contributing factor to some of the relocations in the 1950s was concern over sovereignty, as the United States also had a presence in the Arctic.

Whatever the government's motivations, Inuit discovered that its assurances of jobs and better living conditions were in many cases illusory. Inuit often struggled to adjust to circumstances beyond their control, even though some received benefits from living in settlements, such as less risk in daily life, better health care, and options to work for wages rather than hunt.

Without their dogs, means of transportation and access to good hunting grounds, Inuit in settlements were not able to hunt and provide for their families. These hunter-gatherers who once were self-sufficient became dependent on government handouts. Those who remained in seasonal camps with their dogs and were able to hunt did not starve, while Inuit living in settlements needed cash from wage employment or social benefits to meet their daily needs.

In her book *The Right to be Cold*, Sheila Watt-Cloutier, an Inuk Nobel Prize nominee and one of the world's most recognized environmental and human-rights advocates, writes about John Amagoalik, whose family was part of the government move in the 1950s. Amagoalik was born in a seasonal camp in Arctic Quebec. When he was five years old, his family was forced to move into the High Arctic to form settlements in places like Resolute and Grise Fjord, where the climate was much harsher and survival was a struggle.

"In fact," she writes, "wildlife and other food sources were so scarce, some families had to scavenge from the RCMP garbage for sustenance." Later active in Inuit politics, Amagoalik was instrumental in the creation of Nunavut.

## "Wandering" Dogs

In traditional Inuit life, families used to travel with their dogs, which were considered part of the family, to *ilagiit nunagivaktangit* (seasonal camps) to fish and hunt. When they were not working, dogs were free to roam wherever Inuit set up camp, the way it had been since time immemorial.

When Inuit were relocated to government-established settlements, loose dogs were considered a menace and had to be tied up by order of the Northwest Territories Statutes Dog Act. Based on southern Canadian laws, this ordinance was introduced in 1928, after a local trader's young daughter was killed by two loose dogs belonging to the RCMP.

Inuit did not like tying up their dogs. Tethered dogs were less

When not in harness, Inuit Dogs traditionally roamed free, as depicted in this 1865 illustration of an Inuit village called Oopungnewing near Frobisher Bay on Baffin Island.

active, less vigorous, and did not travel as well as those that were constantly on the move. Inuit believe the simplest way to keep dogs was to let them run loose when they were not in harness. Puppies were never tied up because early human-dog socialization was essential to prevent aggression and teach the dogs to accept humans as dominant. Unsocialized dogs posed a greater threat to humans, whereas dogs that were allowed to forage for food and socialize among themselves were more even tempered. Inuit who grew up with dogs were not afraid of them, unlike many *qallunaat,* who were unfamiliar with dogs.

A devastating distemper outbreak in the early 1960s and diseases such as rabies and canine hepatitis took their toll, decimating thousands of Inuit Dogs in Canada's Eastern Arctic. This was exacerbated by the introduction of snowmobiles, Inuit's move into settlements, a changing lifestyle, and what Inuit call *qimmijaqtauniq,* meaning "the killing of dogs."

## A Vanishing Lifestyle

The introduction of snowmobiles to the Arctic in the 1960s destroyed Inuit's partnership with their dogs. Snowmobiles were

Copper Inuit sled near Cape Krusenstern, NWT (Nunavut). *Credit: Diamond Jennings. Courtesy: Canadian Museum of History.*

CANADIAN INUIT DOG

faster, could travel farther, and required less work than looking after a dog team. However, a Bombardier ski-doo with a 7 hp Kohler engine cost $1,095 in 1961. This effectively excluded nomadic dog team owners, as they would not have been able to afford one.

"In my younger generation it was useful to have a dog team, as they were working dogs," Inuk elder Elijah Padluq reflects. "It was easier for dogs to find their way and avoid getting lost. It is also quieter traveling with dogs. You could see the land better when traveling, as you are going at a good pace, not like snowmobiles, as you are driving at a faster pace. And snowmobiles can run out of gas and break down, and can't find their way back."

In the 1950s and '60s, roaming packs of dogs became an issue, especially in areas where there were many *qallunaat* who were not used to these dogs.

In 1960, longtime Arctic administrator W.G. "Moose" Kerr noted that maulings were an "avoidable risk" in the Arctic.

"From experience in the North I personally do not think that 'Wandering' dogs create any greater hazard than does the

Snowmobiles were faster and could travel farther than Inuit Dogs. Here, one pulls a *qamutiik*, or Inuit-style sled. *Photo: Max Forgues.*

normal automobile traffic of southern Canada," he said. "In the South we warn our children of the necessary safeguards and there is no reason why we can't do the same in the North. It is also my experience that a tied-up dog, if approached by children, is more dangerous than a 'wandering' one."

Warranted or not, thousands of *qimmiit* were killed over several decades by police, bylaw officers, special constables and, according to Ken MacRury, Inuit themselves. While some dogs posed a threat to public safety and were destroyed because they were starving, diseased, abandoned or roaming, others were still in harness or tied up when they were shot.

## Qikiqtani Inuit Association

In 2002 the Qikiqtani Inuit Association (QIA), a non-profit society that represents Inuit in the Qikiqtani (Baffin) region of Nunavut, established a committee to examine the alleged dog killings. QIA started collecting testimonies from Inuit in 2004 and found that the destruction of their *qimmiit* and relocations into government-established settlements after the second World War had "the most profound impact" on Inuit. Stories of "systematic dog killings" pressured the Commons Standing Committee on Aboriginal Affairs and Northern Development to call on the federal government to inquire into the alleged killings of Inuit sled dogs in the North between 1950 and 1970.

The RCMP, which conducted its own investigation, acknowledged many of the killings, but denied they were part of a policy to force Inuit into settlements. According to the RCMP Final Report of May 30, 2006, "the RCMP review team did not uncover any evidence to support the allegations, within the large volume of information collected, of an organized mass slaughter of Inuit sled dogs by RCMP members in Nunavik and Nunavut, between 1950 and 1970." The RCMP concluded its report by stating that "the startling drop in Inuit sled dog populations, particularly during the 1960s," was due to "canine epidemics, the collapse of the fur trade in the late 1940s, the introduction of snowmobiles in the 1960s, the migration of Inuit into settlements, and participation in the market economy rather than living on the land."

Keeping Inuit Dogs tethered is a very new phenomenon; before the mid-20th Century, the dogs were free to roam and forage. *Photo: Kim Han.*

However, what Inuit witnessed and experienced when they lost their dogs was absent from the RCMP report. Critics of the RCMP's self-assessment objected to the small number of individuals interviewed – mostly *qallunaat*. Perhaps not coincidentally, the timing of the killings coincided with the influx of *qallunaat* in the North with the appointment of missionaries, teachers and area administrators, although no specific document has been uncovered that stipulated an official government policy to destroy the Inuit's sled dogs.

## Qikiqtani Truth Commission

In 2007, the Qikiqtani Inuit Association appointed James Igloliorte, a retired judge from Newfoundland and Labrador, to set up the Qikiqtani Truth Commission (QTC) and investigate the alleged dog killings.

The QTC documented three major episodes of dog killings in the Qikiqtani region, which happened in different stages:

The first occurred in Iqaluit, a community in Southern Baffin Island, after 1956, when large numbers of Inuit moved to Iqaluit to work at the airport and a chain of radar stations. According to the QTC report, by the mid-1970s, almost every team of *qimmiit* in Qikiqtaaluk (Baffin Island) had been destroyed. Most killings took place at town dumps, where stray dogs tend to gather; near Distant Early Warning (DEW) line sites where mess-hall waste was dumped; close to trading centers and military stations; on beaches, and on the fringes of a settlement.

Warning sign at dog yard in Iqaluit. *Photo: Kim Han.*

The second major episode of killings took place around Cumberland Sound in 1962, where there was a serious epidemic of canine distemper and hepatitis. To prevent the disease from spreading, the RCMP systematically killed "almost the entire canine population in the region," the report said. Inuit knew that *qimmiit* suffering from rabies have to be killed right away, but they managed diseases such as rabies "mainly by observing and culling sick animals when necessary." Inuit knew they could overcome this adversity, even though it might temporarily reduce the size of their teams and hamper their ability to go hunting. Inuit also knew their teams would regenerate in time. *Qallunaat*, on the other hand, took a different view. They considered a sick *qimmiq* a dangerous *qimmiq*, and a public health risk that should be eliminated.

The third major episode occurred after the construction of schools and the relocation of most Inuit from more than 100 small *ilagiit nunagivaktangit* into 13 permanent communities. Many were not able to keep their dogs and were forced to shoot them before relocating.

In describing his resettlement in a testimony to the QIA in 2004, Pauloosie Ekidlaq recounted how he had to kill his dogs:

"I felt pressured to kill my dogs by the government saying they have better mode of transportation," said Ekidlaq, an Inuk who was relocated to Sanikiluaq, a hamlet on the north coast of Flaherty Island in Hudson Bay. "My dogs were the only way for me to hunt, and to this day this hurts me. There was nobody to kill the dogs like the police so the Inuit were told to kill their own dogs. ... Everybody was shooting their dogs and knew this had to be done because the government was telling them to kill the dogs. As you can imagine, killing all those dogs, shots going off all around and people knowing what is going on. All those dead dogs ..."

Losing their dogs was a traumatic and demoralizing experience that disrupted Inuit lives, traditional values and routines, their means of transportation, hunting practices and means of sustenance. The QTC report revealed that the loss of *qimmiit* also changed Inuit's social standing in the community. Because Inuit considered ownership of large dog teams to be a sign of full manhood, the loss of their dogs destroyed the men's self-worth.

It made them feel useless, because they were no longer able to hunt and provide for their families. In their final report, the RCMP acknowledged that "the demise of the Inuit Sled Dog has come, for many, to symbolize the cultural loss of identity and dignity."

Social and economic changes, combined with the loss of Inuit's hunting companions and changed means of transport to snow machines, resulted in a dramatic decline in dog-sledding culture and maintenance of traditional dogs. In his final report, Commissioner Igloliorte wrote that Inuit who did not have a dog team or snowmobile to access the land for hunting and socializing felt that "life in settlements was a form of imprisonment." It curbed their freedom, and many people were driven to alcohol and gambling, which provided a distraction from boredom and uncertainties about life in general.

"It was evidence of a breakdown of Inuit society ... the switch from our hunting-and-fishing culture to one of trapping and trading," Sheila Watt-Cloutier remarks. She calls it "the wounded hunter spirit ... Years of pent-up anger and frustration caused by the tumultuous changes our people had experienced were finding an outlet in alcohol abuse, addiction and violence."

The QTC Final Report stated that the Canadian government admitted that some dogs were killed, but insisted it was always "justified" for reasons of public health and safety, based on the ordinance that stated that dogs were not permitted to be at large in designated settlements. Unfortunately, the ordinance did not take into consideration cultural practices of Inuit, nor the rules of Inuit society. Inuit elder Simon Idlout of Resolute testified that the laws that were imposed on Inuit were not made in Nunavut and should not apply to them. They were made "down south where the Whites lived."

QTC documented the shootings of more than 400 dogs around the settlement in Pangnirtung in 1966 and '67, noting that by the mid-1970s, almost every dog team had been destroyed.

Witnesses from every settlement had their own stories to tell, about how they witnessed dogs being shot — some while they were in cages, others while tied up — and how some Inuit were coerced into shooting their own dogs when they were forced to move into settlements.

Between January 2008 and May 2009, Commissioner Igloliorte and his staff traveled to 13 communities in the Qikiqtani (Baffin) region to gather testimonies about events between 1950 and 1975 from Inuit who had lived through this difficult period, as well as from their children. The QTC collected testimonies from close to 350 individuals, completed an extensive archival research program, and interviewed *qallunaat* who worked in the region during that period, including a number of retired RCMP officers, government officials and academic researchers.

On October 20, 2010, Commissioner Igloliorte presented the QTC final report, "Achieving *Saimaqatigiingniq*" ("peace between opponents — a relationship in which two opponents meet in the middle and are reconciled") at the QIA's annual meeting. He was quoted as saying "there is a lot of value in ensuring that we accept the oral history that is being presented." He submitted a number of recommendations to improve the relationship between Inuit and the government as two equal partners.

"In order for forgiveness to be given," said John Amagoalik, the Father of Nunavut, "there must be truth and an acknowledgment of what happened."

## More Testimony

In Nunavik, Northern Quebec, the Makivik Corporation, which is the legal representative of Quebec's Inuit, responded to the RCMP's final report by petitioning the Quebec government to conduct an independent inquiry into the "dog slaughters" in

Nunavik in the 1950s and 1960s. In November 2007, Quebec and Makivik appointed retired Superior Court of Quebec Judge Jean-Jacques Croteau to visit 14 Nunavik communities to gather testimonies from persons who witnessed the dog killings of the 1950s and '60s or were affected by them. He questioned 179 witnesses, read 76 interview transcripts, and examined numerous archival and historical documents, including the RCMP's 2006 report.

In his findings, Judge Croteau determined that one of the main reasons for the killing of dogs was strays. "In the whole of Nunavik, the attacks of dogs on peoples [sic] mainly took place in the villages and not in camps," he wrote. "Children were most often the victims of these attacks." He underscored the lack of communication between Inuit and "white peoples," as both had "differing rules and beliefs regarding the dogs that led to animosity between the two groups."

Judge Croteau also documented epidemics of diseases that decimated the canine population in the Kuujuaq region in 1959 and 1960, and on the Hudson Bay coast in 1961 and 1962. In order to protect the dogs and contain disease, the federal government sent hundreds of doses of vaccines to various communities in Nunavik. Judge Croteau found that people were able to regenerate the loss of dogs due to illness over a number of years. But he also noted that dogs were killed by RCMP officers between 1950 and 1960. Some were shot, others poisoned or gassed. Judge Croteau reported how two witnesses told of two provincial officers who arrived in Kangiqsujuaq by seaplane. After disembarking, they started chasing and shooting stray dogs in the village without saying a word. "They killed 32 of them and simply left thereafter without explanation."

Although "nothing in the file" led Judge Croteau to believe there was a "systematic elimination" of sled dogs, he and his team estimated that "approximately 1,000 healthy dogs were killed."

Based on facts reported by Inuit, the judge believed that

"provincial authorities and officers had a total lack of awareness of the culture of the Inuit and [their] relationship to natural resources, the land, the climate, the environment and finally their companions, the sled dogs."

In March 2010, Judge Croteau submitted his final report, which concluded that "the federal government did slaughter hundreds of sled dogs in order to force Inuit into community settlements in Nunavik." As a result, he wrote, "the whole of Nunavik society suffered damaging consequences from the actions, attitudes and mistakes of bureaucrats, agents and representatives of the two governments who killed at least 1,000 dogs in Nunavik during the 1950s and 1960s."

Inuit elders from Nunavik who experienced the dog slaughters from the late 1950s through the early 1970s, at the 2005 premiere of "Echo of the Last Howl," a documentary about that troubled time. *Photo: Isabelle Dubois/Makivik.*

In 2011, Quebec Premier Jean Charest made a formal apology to the Inuit of Nunavik in recognition of the dog slaughter on behalf of the government of Quebec. Commemorative plaques were installed in each of the 14 Inuit communities in Nunavik to memorialize the tragedy. The Quebec government also pledged $3 million to support Nunavimmiut (the people of Nunavik) whose dogs were killed between 1950 and 1975. On the recommendation of Judge Croteau, part of this compensation was to be used "to organize sled-dog races in Nunavik, promote the sale of Inuit art and sculptures, and promote the teaching and use of Inuktitut and syllabics in Nunavik."

# A Plan for Preservation

**An ambitious breed-recovery project helps revive the Inuit Dog**

C anada's Arctic was once home to an estimated 20,000 "Eskimo Dogs," the name by which the Inuit Dog was previously known. Between 1960 and 1970, there were reportedly only a few hundred left.

John McGrath, an economic development officer with the government of the Northwest Territories, observed that, with the

arrival of snowmobiles, Eskimo Dogs in Spence Bay and other nearby communities started disappearing. When McGrath met Bill Carpenter in Spence Bay in 1972, both men were concerned about the precipitous decline of Eskimo Dogs. Based on their observations in the North, Carpenter and McGrath knew that this breed existed, but, according to Carpenter, "in the dog world, very few people had even heard of the dog."

That's when both men decided that something needed to be done to save what Carpenter refers to as "this distinctly Arctic breed called Eskimo," especially, because "the status of this dog in the rest of Canada was virtually unknown."

Carpenter contacted kennel clubs in Canada and the United States to track down breeders. They reported they no longer had registered "Eskimo Dogs." Carpenter started researching the Eskimo Dog and discovered that several specimens were obtained from Canada's Arctic in the late 1800s, when there was no question as to their authenticity. He found that the Eskimo Dog, which had gone through several name changes, had been listed with the Canadian Kennel Club since 1891. According to Carpenter, "this registered line continued to exist and, with a few new additions from Arctic Canada, had survived as a pure breed under Canada's National Livestock Pedigree Act which, for dogs, was administered by the Canadian Kennel Club (CKC)."

As far as records of the CKC were concerned, however, the breed was gone, as there were no active breeders. In the United States, the American Kennel Club removed "Eskimo Dog" from its list of recognized Working breeds in the late 1950s, because none had been registered for years.

In 1976, the CKC advised Carpenter that the last litter of registered Eskimo Dogs had been born in 1966. Further investigation revealed that the only registered dog that was alive was a sterile male. This prompted Carpenter and McGrath to take action.

In 1972, Carpenter and McGrath established the William J. Carpenter Canadian Eskimo Dog Research Foundation (CEDRF) in Yellowknife, Northwest Territories (NWT), with assistance from Canadian and territorial governments. Their aim was to restore the dwindling numbers of Eskimo Dogs. The foundation was supported by Inuit, who acknowledged the dramatic decline in the numbers of their indigenous dog. At that time the Inuit Cultural Society of the NWT, which was located in Eskimo Point, sanctioned the renaming of the dog from "Eskimo" to "Canadian Eskimo Dog," as long as "Qimmiq" was included in the breed standard.

In January 1998, McGrath, who was a member of the Canadian Kennel Club's Breed Standard Committee for the Eskimo Dog and president of the Eskimo Dog Society of the NWT, made a presentation to the Yankee Alaskan Malamute Club annual meeting in Massachusetts about the disappearance of Eskimo Sled Dogs. He spoke of "the genesis of the Eskimo Dog Project" with Bill Carpenter. It was a plan to "consolidate knowledge about the Eskimo Dog and, if possible, start a breeding program which would lead to re-registration of the Eskimo Dog with the CKC."

Carpenter and McGrath reviewed early archival photographs, the CKC breed standard for the Eskimo Dog and numerous scientific papers, including an 1827 article by J.G. Children, "On the Esquimaux Dog." They also reviewed a 1924 paper by American zoologist Glover Morrill Allen entitled "Dogs of the American Aborigines," considered the earliest definitive work on the topic. Both men also consulted Inuit elders to determine what the phenotypically best specimens should look like. CEDRF then created a breeding program using only Canadian breeding stock from Inuit of northern Canada.

*Opposite page: A charming duo. Photo: Siu-Ling Han.*

In the early to mid-1970s, CEDRF purchased 41 of the phenotypically best specimens out of approximately 200 Eskimo dogs remaining in various remote camps and settlements such as Resolute Bay, Somerset Island, Spence

Bay, Hall Beach and Repulse Bay. Carpenter obtained more good stock from the Inummarit Cultural Society in Igloolik, an Inuit hamlet in Foxe Basin, north of the Arctic Circle, close to the Melville Peninsula.

"The greatest contribution to this project came from Inuit who owned some of the best Eskimo dogs in the Canadian North," Carpenter notes.

Carpenter had opened a boarding kennel in Yellowknife, NWT, and brought in a part-time veterinarian. For the nominal annual rent of $25, the city provided a large property where CEDRF was able to build large pens.

"Following the advice of Dr. Roy Crawford of the University of Saskatchewan, a specialist in rare breeds and rare gene stock, CEDRF randomly selected one male and one female from each litter for the next breeding generation, making sure parentage was properly documented," Carpenter explains. "This process was carefully recorded through three generations. The end result was a line of registered dogs that bred true to type. The only requirement was that all dogs in the program prove themselves to be good working sled dogs. Dogs that were not kept from the random selection were returned to various Inuit outpost camps, free of charge."

MacRury comments that "most returned dogs were dead within a year or crossbred to mongrels." Why? It's difficult to answer, but possibly the grief and trauma of losing their dogs were still too fresh in many Inuit's minds to start a breeding program.

Meanwhile, breeders were set up across Canada and provided with CKC-registered Canadian Eskimo Dogs as breeding stock.

"The future of the breed is in the hands of registered breeders who document parentage," Carpenter notes, but, "culturally, it is in the hand of Northerners that keep and use the dogs as they were historically meant to be used.

"Qimmiq ... deserves at least a place in modern Canada, and should not be forced into extinction," Carpenter concludes. "The future of this dog is not with southern dog shows, not with pet owners on leashes."

In appreciation of Carpenter's initiative and hard work to save *qimmiit*, visiting elders from the Inuit Cultural Society of the Northwest Territories wrote Carpenter's Inuit nickname — Qimmiliriji — in Inuktitut syllabics. *Qimmiliriji* means "The Dog Man."

A decade after Carpenter and McGrath started the CEDRF, most of the dogs they had in Yellowknife were registered with the CKC. It was, as Carpenter wrote, "time to wind down the large breeding program." With support from the government of the Northwest Territories, CEDRF dispatched kennel-club-registered Canadian Eskimo Dogs to breeders in the NWT, Yukon, British Columbia, Alberta, Manitoba, Ontario and Quebec, marking an end to a long and successful breeding program to save the breed from extinction.

Canadian Eskimo Dogs from Carpenter's breeding program in 1999. *Photos: Sue Hamilton.*

# Return of the Inuit Dog

## Back in the harness and ready to run

As people began to acknowledge the historical and cultural significance of the Inuit Dog in the life of Inuit, enthusiasts in Nunavut and Nunavik started to establish events to preserve its role as a northern sled dog.

The Inuit Dog's continued existence as a working dog, however, is tenuous, as the number of traditional Inuit Dogs in the Arctic continues to decline, due in part to unintentional crossbreeding. "I can honestly say that most of the dogs in Nunavik are contaminated with other breeds," says Allen Gordon, an Inuk in Nunavik and veteran of Ivakkak races since 2010.

Gordon says there is no controlled breeding program in Nunavik, though he notes that some mushers imported pure Inuit Sled Dogs from Greenland. He tells the story of a musher from Greenland named Ono who went to Nunavik on numerous expeditions in the 1990s, leaving his teams with a number of people in some villages at the end of his trips. As a result, Gordon says, "the pure breed came back somewhat," though he adds that "most of the younger people do not even know purity that well. If it looks like a husky with straight-up ears, it's a husky. That's about it."

Although there is no organized breeding program in Nunavik, owners of Inuit Dog teams in Nunavut and Nunavik have been

*On the preceding page:* Aerial view of Allen Gordon's dog team during the 2004 Ivakkak race. *Photo: Pierre Dunnigan. ©Makivik.*

working together to increase the number of authentic Inuit Dogs. They try to maintain the working ability and performance of these dogs, based on strength and endurance.

# Pangaggujjiniq Nunavut Quest

When the largest aboriginal land-claim agreement in Canadian history, known as the James Bay and Northern Quebec Agreement (JBNQA), was signed in 1975, and Nunavut became an official territory of Canada in 1999, Inuit could take control of their communities and basic services such as education, health, social and economic development policies, and the administration of justice. It also gave Inuit equal representation with the government in the management of wildlife, resources and the environment.

A group of Inuit on northern Baffin Island in Arctic Bay decided they had to do

## SETTLING DOWN

When Quebec announced the James Bay Hydro-electric development in James Bay in 1971, the rights of the Cree and Inuit who lived in Northern James Bay were not taken into consideration. A group of Inuit under the leadership of Charlie Watt, an Inuk leader, hunter and businessman, founded the Norther Québec Inuit Association (NQIA) and, together with the Quebec Association of Indians (QAI), they applied for an injunction to stop the project, which would encroach on their lands. After two years of court cases, and intense and difficult negotiations with the government of Canada, and Quebec, the James Bay Energy Corporation, the James Bay Development Corporation and Hydro Quebec, an out-of-court settlement was reached. That became the historic James Bay and Northern Quebec Agreement (JBNQA), the largest land-claim agreement in the history of Canada.

something to celebrate the creation of their new territory and self-government, and the Inuit tradition of dog teaming.

According to the Nunavut Quest website, Moses Ujukuluk, Cecil Marshall, Joeli Qamanirq, Piuyuq Enoogoo and Niore Iqalukjuak decided to hold a sled-dog race in which only Inuit Dogs were to be used. Siberian Huskies or Alaska racing dogs were not allowed. Anyone was allowed to enter, as long as they used not fewer than 10 and not more than 12 traditional Inuit Dogs per team. Participants had to use a *qamutiik* that was not less than ten feet and not more than twelve feet long. The dogs had to

Lee Inuaak and dogs on the Nunavut Quest. *Photo: Clare Kines.*

run in a traditional fan hitch, tethered to the sled on separate traces measuring 14 to 40 feet (4.5 and 12 meters) in length.

The first race, which started on April 13, 1999, was called the "North Baffin Quest." Fifteen *qimuksiktiit* (dog drivers) from various communities on Baffin Island took off from Arctic Bay and headed to Igloolik, a distance of 276 miles (445 kilometers), with 180 sled dogs. The competing *qimuksiktiit* came from Arctic Bay, Clyde River, Hall Beach, Igloolik and Pond Inlet.

Since then, this marathon racing event has been called the Pangaggujjiniq Nunavut Quest. It starts in March or April of each year, at a time when Arctic weather conditions can be severe and unpredictable. Participants may have to brave blinding blizzards, huge winds and cracking sea ice. They also have to beware of polar bears.

According to its official rules, which started with four rules but increased to 32 over the years, the Nunavut Quest is for long-distance working sled dogs, not sprinters. Participants must be totally self-sufficient and ready for any emergency. They have to carry all the required supplies on their *qamutiik*, including a snow saw and knife (for emergency igloo construction), a two-burner camp stove, food and a rifle. The sledge used in the Nunavut Quest must be a traditional *qamutiik*, and all dog harnesses, whips and traces must be handmade.

The starting and finishing points for this race alternate between various totally isolated North Baffin communities in the Eastern Arctic. There is no official pre-determined race map or written route, and no set trails or directional markers. A general route is discussed and sometimes a map is consulted, but according to Shari Fox Gearheard of Clyde River, Nunavut, who

Jake Gearheard winning the 2015 Nunavut Quest. *Photo: Clare Kines.*

has participated in several Nunavut Quests with her husband Jake, "the knowledge of the race leaders and elders, weather, traditional campsites, ice conditions and other factors dictate the exact daily route and locations for each day and where we camp each night."

Onlookers keeping an eye out for race participants. *Photo: Clare Kines.*

It takes from seven to ten days to complete the approximately 250 miles (400 kilometers) of the tour, depending on the route, number of checkpoints, weather and ice conditions encountered on the trail. There is no veterinary or medical presence, and no sophisticated support system; just family and friends driving at least one snow-machine per team to tow all the supplies needed for travel, camp, and food for people and dogs. A local elder or expert hunter leads the support-crew convoy as they set off one hour ahead of the racers, traveling roughly 50 miles (80 kilometers) each day, to set up the end of day's camp.

The Nunavut Quest is a social and cultural event to celebrate the Inuit Dog and dog teaming. Participants from different communities come together to run and "race" their dogs, socialize with friends and family, and share stories, fun and food, traditional Inuit knowledge, and land and navigational skills, as well as dog-teaming skills. It highlights the strong working relationship between *qimuksiktiit* and their dogs. When the teams stop for a tea break on the trail, they share training and feeding techniques, and point out good hunting areas to each other. At the end of the race there is often an exchange of dogs between communities in order to share blood lines.

The Nunavut Quest commemorates a time when traveling by dog team was a way of life. It is about the courage, patience and determination of ancestral Inuit who managed to thrive and survive in the harsh, unforgiving Arctic.

## Ivakkak Sled Dog Race

In 2000, the Makivik Corporation decided to organize Nunavik's own dog-team race with a portion of the money from the compensation provided by the Quebec government for the loss of Nunavik dogs, as specified by Judge Croteau. Makivik, which means "to rise up," encourages Nunavimmiut (inhabitants of Nunavik) to revive the practice of dog sledding. One year later, Ivakkak was born.

The first Ivakkak race was held March 28, 2001. It was named

Allen Gordon and team approach the finish line at the 2004 Ivakkak race. *Photo: Pierre Dunnigan.* ©*Makivik.*

Ivakkak, an Inuktitut word meaning "when the dogs are at their best," by Johnny Watt, a well-known dog-sled master and former mayor of Kangiqsualujjuaq in Nunavik. The Ivakkak is an annual long-distance dog-sledding race traversing various Nunavik communities. It covers an average of 375 miles (600 kilometers).

Like the Nunavut Quest, it is organized to celebrate Inuit culture, promote the traditional way of dog sledding, and celebrate the return of traditional Inuit Dogs to Nunavik from near extinction. Dogs participating in the race are subjected to strict scrutiny to ensure they are traditional "Inuit Husky Dogs." But, unlike the Nunavut Quest, participation in the Ivakkak race is limited to Inuit of Nunavik, 16 years and older, and beneficiaries of the James Bay and Northern Quebec Agreement.

One of Ivakkak's most celebrated participants is Harry Okpik, a 63-year-old champion dog sledder from Quaqtaq, Nunavik. Okpik was 11 years old when he witnessed the dog killings, which had a devastating effect on him. As a boy, it was his wish to one day own his father's dogs, but that was not to be. "I remember very well the dog slaughter," he says. "We heard gunshots all day."

When Okpik was 22 years old, he accidentally shot his leg in a hunting accident that almost killed him. He spent two years in a Montreal hospital with no prospect for recovery and finally decided to have his leg amputated. It took years, a lot of hard work and determination for Okpik to overcome his disability and, as he says, "make something of my life." He has participated in at least ten Ivakkak races and become a role model for the disabled. "If I go dog-sledding," he says, "I feel like an Inuk." In a 2015 interview with the Canadian Broadcasting Company, Okpik said: "My dogs have helped me tremendously ... They have made my life whole."

# Qimualaniq Quest

The Qimualaniq Quest, which began in 2007, was a challenging 200-mile (320-kilometer) dog-sledding race from Iqaluit to Kimmirut and back. It was organized by Nunavut's Francophone Association and Kimmirut's Mayukalik Hunters and Trappers Association to revitalize dog sledding with traditional Inuit Dogs on Baffin Island. The Qimualaniq Quest was considered an opportunity for Inuit and French and English Canadians living in the North to get together and celebrate living in the Arctic.

Participants had to carry two 40-kilogram bags of flour for a total of 80 kilograms (176 pounds) on their *qamutiik* to recall the olden

Siu-Ling Han participating in the Qimualaniq Quest. *Photo: Fred Lemire.*

days, when dog teams carried all their supplies and game. In addition to the flour, which was used in a feast to welcome the *qimuksiktiit*, each participant also had to carry a sleeping bag and tent, and enough supplies to last at least two days.

After two years, the 2009 Qimualaniq Quest was cancelled due to lack of funding and has not been run since.

# Qimmivut

Qimmivut, which means "our dogs" in Inuktitut, is about passing on Inuit land skills, values and knowledge, and Inuit relationships with dogs. It is an annual land-based program organized by the Ilisaqsivik Society of Clyde River, Nunavut, with support from various funders. Qimmivut provides young people with an opportunity to be out on the land with recognized hunters, dog-team owners and elders.

"Qimmivut is an example of how, for Inuit, dog teaming is more than dog teaming. Working with dogs is at the heart of Inuit culture and the knowledge needed for working with dogs is rich and, in so many ways, deeply meaningful to those who practice it," Jake Gearheard, executive director of the Ilisaqsivik Society,

Inuit man and boy working on a dog sled, place and date unknown. Joseph Vincent Jacobsen collection. *Courtesy Library and Archives Canada.*

explains. "Passing this knowledge and practice on to youth today is not only about giving them the skills to run their own working dogs, travel and hunt, but also the ability to transfer the many skills they learn to all aspects of living a good, healthy life."

Qimmivut promotes the development of mentoring relationships between elders, adults and youth. Youngsters learn about caring for and working with dogs; traveling by dog team, and about the social, economic and cultural significance of dogs. They also learn how to make harnesses, leads, whips and backpacks. Elders share traditional knowledge around practical navigation, winter travel and camping skills; tool-making and harvesting skills, and environmental stewardship, as well as social values like working with others in harmony.

Qimmivut also has "Father and Son on the Land" programs in which men and boys spend time on the land with dogs to go hunting and fishing. The boys are taught hunting and rifle-handling skills, net-making and tool-making. They also learn the history of the areas they visit, and the meanings and stories of traditional place names. In bad weather conditions, they learn how to stay safe, how to create a shelter to weather the storm, and how to be patient and pass the time productively, as they bond with their elders — and dogs.

Organizers and participants of the Pangaggujjiniq Nunavut Quest and Ivakkak dog sled races are to be commended for their enthusiasm, commitment and support to bring back the traditional Inuit Dog — the kind of dog their ancestors used to have, and the Inuit tradition of dog teaming that was crucial in the survival of their ancestors. Since the first Nunavut Quest in 1999 and the first Ivakkak Race in 2001, both events have grown into a popular winter tradition in Nunavut and Nunavik.

"We continue to see the youth and the elders active in this lifestyle," Andy Moorhouse, vice president of economic development for the Makivik Corporation, told *Nunatsiaq Online*, "and we believe we are reaching our ultimate goal, to ensure the return of *qimmituinnaq*, the Inuit sled dog, which was vital to Inuit survival across the North."

# Today's Canadian Inuit Dog

Ensuring this icon of Inuit life survives for future generations

Today, Inuit Dogs are not only used to revive and preserve an ancient culture and tradition. They are also used in sport hunting and recreation, and as a means to promote eco-tourism and adventure tourism in the changing Arctic.

As an icon for Arctic travel, the Inuit Dog attracts visitors from around the world who long for an adventure in a mystical world far removed from their own, where the spirits of Arctic explorers, the hardy, the bold and the brave, still roam. As for Inuit, the dogs are a reminder of the strength, resourcefulness and tenacity of their ancestors, whose lives were intertwined with them for survival in one of the harshest environments on earth.

Thanks to CEDRF, Makivik, Qimmivut, the Ilisaqsivik Society of Clyde River; people like Moses Ujukuluk, Cecil Marshall, Joeli Qamanirq, Piuyuq Enoogoo and Niore Iqalukjuak, who initiated the North Baffin Quest before it became known as the Nunavut Quest; Harry Okpik and fellow dog sledders in Nunavik, and the many Inuit and non-Inuit devoted to the preservation of this unique landrace in its native habitat and all over the world, the future of the Inuit Dog as a symbol of Canada's northern history will, hopefully, be preserved for future generations.

*On the preceding page:* Time to go. *Photo: Debbie McAllister.*

This amazing dog asked for little but gave so much in return. He assisted with the hunt and was a loyal companion and protector.

He kept him warm when needed. He worked hard, pulling heavily laden sledges across the frozen tundra in all kinds of weather and back home safely.

When asked if he thought that it was important for Inuit Dog teams to continue working in the North, Elijah didn't think so. "The way of life is not the same as it used to be," he explained. As for his vision and hope for the next generation of Inuit and sled dogs, he found that difficult to define. "The dogs that are used now are not the same dogs we used before, and we worked with our dogs each and every day."

While it may be impossible to recapture the past, organizations such as Qimmivut are to be commended for revitalizing dog teaming, and the culture, knowledge and skills to work with traditional dogs that were instrumental in the survival of Inuit's ancestors for thousands of years.

Times have changed, but there are people who try to uphold what the Inuit Dog represents: friendship, cooperation, strength, resilience, courage and enduring loyalty. The Inuit Dog needs to be cherished, treasured, worked and bred to the highest standards to maintain its blood line and function as a working sled dog in its natural environment — the circumpolar north.

The Inuit Dog epitomizes Canada's Arctic culture and embodies the past, present and future as Canada's historical and national treasure, an icon of Canada's North.

*He is your friend, your partner, your defender, your dog. You are his life, his love, his leader. He will be yours, faithful and true, to the last beat of his heart. You owe it to him to be worthy of such devotion.* — **Unknown**

Resting dog, Pangnirtung, Nunavut, January 1946. *Photo: Bud Glunz, National Film Board of Canada.*

# Acknowledgments

A thank-you to those who helped make this book possible

F iction or non-fiction? That was my choice for my last assignment for a course I took at the Institute for Children's Literature. I decided on non-fiction because I love research.

After visiting my daughter, Siu-Ling, in Iqaluit, I became acquainted with her Inuit Dogs and their captivating personalities. That's when Siu-Ling suggested I write about the Inuit Dog. Apart from Geneviève Montcombroux's *The Canadian Inuit Dog: Canada's Heritage*, first published in 1997, I had not come across any books that focused on the Canadian Inuit Dog.

Siu-Ling suggested that I visit *The Fan Hitch* web site. Bingo! I found all kinds of information about the Inuit Dog, including scholarly articles and news items. The more I read, the greater my enthusiasm to delve into the history of these amazing dogs. I had romantic notions of dogs pulling sleds in a wintry landscape but did not realize that, without their dogs, Inuit would not have been able to survive in one of the harshest environments on earth. Nothing romantic about that!

*On the preceding page: Inuit Dog siblings. Photo: Shari Fox Gearheard.*

Then I read Mark Hamilton's review of *Polar Dream* in *The Fan Hitch*. Helen Thayer, a 50-year-old adventurer and explorer, was the first woman to make a solo journey to the magnetic North Pole without resupply. Fiercely independent, she at first refused to bring dogs with her, but when Inuit hunters warned her of the danger of polar bears she agreed to take one to protect her. I was fascinated by the relationship that developed between Thayer and the Inuit Husky she named Charlie. Although Charlie was not a pure Inuit Dog, he had its instincts and qualities, loyally accompanying her across the barren landscape, in all kinds of weather. He saved her from being attacked by a polar bear and from falling through cracking sea ice. Thayer's description of Charlie made me want to learn more. That is how my book came to be, but I could not have done it on my own.

Jessica Lee Anderson, my instructor at the Institute of Children's Literature, was the first person who read my finished assignment. "I viewed [your manuscript] as a gift waiting under the Christmas tree. I couldn't wait

The author and friends. *Photo: Jeff Han.*

to open it, but wanted to cherish it once I did," she wrote me. "I hope you feel quite proud of yourself for the blood, sweat and tears you've poured into this project."

Blood, sweat and tears, indeed. It's taken me more than eight years to get this far. I owe my deepest gratitude to my beloved daughter Siu-Ling, who introduced me to real Inuit Dogs and shared her love and enthusiasm for them. Siu-Ling went over my manuscripts numerous times, explained things to me, made suggestions, comments and corrections, and always kept encouraging me when I was overwhelmed and about to give up.

A great big thank-you to my husband, Bing, for putting up with my many late nights in front of the computer. To my sons Jeff and Tim, thanks for your love and support when times were tough.

I thank my publisher and editor, Denise Flaim, who believed in me and considered this book worth publishing. Her patience and guidance are much appreciated. Although my dear Siu-Ling won't see my book in print, I am grateful that she at least was able to hold my contract in her hands. It brought a smile to her face when she told me how happy she was, and how proud it made her, before giving me a big hug and a daughterly pat on my back.

There are so many friends to thank. Ken MacRury, a dear old friend of Siu-Ling's, patiently reviewed my manuscript numerous times. Ken made comments, corrections and suggestions, as did Sue and Mark Hamilton of *The Fan Hitch*, who were more than generous with their help and provided me with all kinds of information and photographs. I thank Ken and the Hamiltons for putting up with my many questions and requests to check and verify things I had written, as well as Siu-Ling's dog-sledding friends who took the time to go over my manuscript, and share their experiences with me: Paul Crowley, Lynn Peplinski, Matty McNair, Andrew Maher, Shari Fox Gearheard, Sarah and Eric McNair-Landry and, of course, Allen Gordon, who took the time out of his busy schedule to write the foreword.

I must not forget Qimmiliriji, the "Dog Man," Bill Carpenter, who kindly reviewed my manuscript and related his story about the creation of the Canadian Eskimo Dog Research Foundation (CEDRF), and his life and experience with "Eskimo" Dogs.

My thanks also go to polar explorer Brent Boddy for sharing his observations of Inuit Dogs and polar huskies, and to Beverley Arseneau, who gave me insight into breeding and rearing purebred Canadian Eskimo Dogs south of the Arctic.

Chris Douglas of Pirurvik provided linguistic advice about the use of Inuktitut words. Lynn Peplinski consulted an Inuk colleague, Seporah Ungalaq, about the correct spelling and translation of

Inuktitut words. I thank all of them for taking the time out of their busy lives.

Thanks to Peter Savolainen, Natalia Rybczybski and Xiaoming Wang for clarifying science that went over my head.

Nathalie Mathieu of Library and Archives Canada and Erin Gurski and Vincent Lafond of the Canadian Museum of History helped with my request for archival photographs. Debbie McAllister, one of Siu-Ling's closest friends who was on the Baffin expedition with her, provided many photos and information about the Baffin trip. Many of Siu-Ling's friends in Nunavut and elsewhere generously shared their photos with me: Madeleine Cole, Matty McNair, Paul Crowley, Thomas Godfrey, Shari Fox Gearheard, Allen Gordon, Isabelle Dubois, Elise Maltinsky and, last but not least, Mark and Sue Hamilton.

My thanks also go out to the professional photographers who have been very generous in sharing their beautiful photos with me. Mike Beedell's overhead photo of a running team graces the background of our cover. Fred Lemire of Iqaluit and Ed Maruyama gave us beautiful photos of Siu-Ling and her team, and Pierre Dunnigan kindly provided pictures of the Ivakkak race. A special thank-you to Clare Kines of Arctic Bay, who kindly shared his wonderful Nunavut Quest photos with me.

Kari Herbert shared a painting by her explorer-father Wally Herbert, and Looqi Schmidt sent photos of his Greenland Dogs. I also included a watercolor by Inuk artist Germaine Arnaktauyok.

What would this book be without the story of a real Inuk? This book also honors Inuk elder Elijah Padluq, a brave polar-bear hunter who traveled and hunted with a team of Inuit Dogs before the invention of snowmobiles. To Kathy Martha Padluq, who helped with the translation when I interviewed her father, Elijah, my heartfelt thanks. I salute Elijah and all Inuit hunters who braved the dangers and the elements of a polar climate to hunt and provide for their families, the way their ancestors did, in the mists of time.

# Resources

More information about the Canadian Inuit Dog

*Echo of the Last Howl.* (DVD) January 2005 documentary produced by Taqramiut Productions. For information: Makivik Corporation, Kuujjuaq. P.O. Box 179, Kuujjuaq, Quebec, J0M 1C0; (819) 964-2925; 1-877-625-4845. www.youtube.com/watch?v=IpHPH4VYKAA

*The Fan Hitch.* A digital meeting place to search for information and share experiences and expertise on the aboriginal/traditional Inuit Dog of the circumpolar north. It also includes information about Inuit culture and tradition. www.thefanhitch.org/resources.html

*The Inuit Dog. Its Provenance, Environment and History.* Master's thesis of Ian Kenneth MacRury. Scott Polar Research Institute. University of Cambridge. Available through *The Fan Hitch* website: www.thefanhitch.org

*Ilisaqsiviq Society.* Non-profit Inuit organization in Clyde River, Nunavut, dedicated to promoting community wellness by providing space, resources and programming. www.ilisaqsivit.ca

*Interim report: Allegations concerning the slaughter of sled dogs.* Submitted by The Honourable Jean-Jacques Croteau, Retired Judge of the Superior Court, to the Makivik Corporation.

*Makivik Corporation:* Makivik, which means "to rise up" in Inuktitut, is mandated to protect the rights and interests of Inuit of Nunavik, and to manage the financial compensation provided by the 1975 James Bay and Northern Quebec Agreement (JBNQA). www.makivik.org

Makivik. SUBMISSION. To the Minister of Indian and Northern Affairs for the Government of Canada and to the Ministère délégué aux Affaires autochtones for the Government of Quebec regarding the Slaughtering of Nunavut "Qimmiit" from the mid-1950s to the late 1960s.

*Okpik's Dream.* DVD. A man and his sled dogs. www.okpiksdream.com.

*Primitive Aboriginal Dog Society International* (PADS). Moscow-based organization whose goal is to facilitate communication

*On the preceding page: An inuksuk, or structure of roughly stacked stones, in Gjoa Haven, Nunavut Photo: J. Warren.*

between scientists and others who are interested in primitive and aboriginal dogs. www.padsociety.org

*Qikiqtani Inuit Association* (QIA). Non-profit Inuit organization representing Inuit in the Qikiqtani (Baffin) region of Nunavut. It represents 13 communities from Grise Fiord in the High Arctic down to Sanikiluaq (Belcher Island). www.QIA.ca

*Qikiqtani Truth Commission* (QTC). Created by the Qikiqtani Inuit Association (QIA) in October 2007 to investigate facts, interview witnesses and hold public hearings on the alleged dog slaughter, as well as relocation. https://qia.ca/qia-expands-qikiqtani-truth-commission-website/

*QTC. Interview and Testimony Summaries.* Submitted October 20, 2010 at the board meeting of the Qikiqtani Inuit Association.

Qikiqtani Truth Commission. *Thematic reports and Special Studies 1950-1975. Qimmiliriniq: Inuit Sled Dogs in Qikiqtaaluk.* Iqaluit, Nunavut 2013. www.qtcommission.ca/.../thematic_reports_english_qimmiliriniq.pdf

*QTC Final Report: Achieving Saimaqatinqiingniq.* Iqaluit, Nunavut 2013. www.qtcommission.ca/en/reports/thematic-reports-and-special-studies-1950-1975

*Qimmit: A Clash of Two Truths.* (DVD) Ole Gjerstad and Joelie Sanguya. Produced by National Film Board of Canada and Piksuk Media. www.nfb.ca/film/qimmit-clash_of_two_truths/

*Qimmivut.* A workshop devoted to nurturing the relationship between Inuit youth, young adults and their dogs. http://ilisaqsivik.ca/programs-and-services/land-based-programming/qimmivut

Royal Canadian Mounted Police. *FINAL REPORT: RCMP Review of Allegations Concerning Inuit Sled Dogs.* 2006-05-30. www.thefanhitch.org/officialreports/RCMPFinal.pdf

# Bibliography

Sources and background material

Achenbach, Joel. "Genes show mysterious Paleo-Eskimos survived 4,000 years until sudden demise." *Washington Post*, August 28, 2014.

Aldhebiani, Amal. Department of Biological Science. King Abdul Aziz University. "Species Concept Speciation." *Saudi Journal of Biological Sciences.* Vol. 25 (3), March 2018. pp. 437 – 440.

Anderson, Eric. *Canada's Relationship with Inuit: A History of Policy and Program Development.* Indigenous and Northern Affairs Canada website. www.aadnc-aandc.gc.ca.

Avery, Tom. *To the end of the Earth: Our epic journey to the North Pole and the legend of Peary and Henson.* New York, NY: St. Martin's Press. 2009.

Backhouse, Constance. Colour-coded. *A Legal History of Racism in Canada, 1900-1950.* Osgoode Society for Canadian Legal History. University of Toronto Press. 1999.

Baines, Becky with Dr. Gary Weitzman. *Everything Dogs.* Washington, DC: National Geographic Society. 2012.

Barr, William. "The Use of Dog Sledges during the British Search for the Missing Franklin Expedition in the North American Arctic Islands, 1848 - 1859." *ARCTIC.* Vol. 62, No. 3 (September 2009), pp. 257-272.

BBC. *Greenland by dog sledge. The Sirius patrol in numbers.* Nov. 30, 2011.

Bennett, John. "Qitdlarssuaq." *Canadian Encyclopedia.*

Beregovoy, Vladimir. "Evolutionary Changes in Domesticated Dogs: The Broken Covenant of the Wild." *Fan Hitch. Journal of the Inuit Sled Dog International.* Part I in *Vol. 11, No.2* (March. 2009). Part II. Vol. 11, No. 3 (June 2009). Part III in Vol. 11, No. 4 (September 2009).

"The Concept of an Aboriginal Dog Breed." *The Fan Hitch.* Vol. 15, No. 3 (June 2013).

Bidner, Jenny. *Is My Dog A Wolf? How Your Pet Compares to its WILD Cousin.* New York, NY: Lark Books. 2006.

Blix, Arnoldus Schytte. *Arctic Animals and their Adaptations to Life on the Edge.* Trondheim: Tapir Academic Press. 2005.

Bown, Stephen R. *White Eskimo. Knud Rasmussen's Fearless Journey into the Heart of the Arctic.* Madeira Park, B.C.: Douglas McIntyre Ltd. 2015.

Boyko, Adam R. et al. "Complex Population Structure in African Village Dogs and its Implications for Inferring Dog Domestication History." *Proceedings of the National Academy of Sciences.* Vol. 106, No. 33 (August 18, 2009), pp. 13903-13908.

Brazeau, Mark. "Defining the Inuit Dog." *The Fan Hitch.* Vol. 9, No. 1 (December 2006).

Brooke, James. "In Far North, Fabled Dogs Come Bounding Back." *The New York Times.* January 31, 2001.

Brown, Sarah K. *Anthropology and Veterinary Genetics.* University of

*On the preceding page: "Hunting the Polar Bear," wood engraving, published in Harper's Weekly Newspaper, 1868.*

California. Davis. "Antiquity of the Inuit Sled Dog Supported by Recent DNA Studies." *The Fan Hitch*. Vol. 15, No. 2 (March, 2013).

Brown, Sarah K., et al. "Ancient DNA Evidence for Genetic Continuity in Arctic Dogs." *Journal of Archaeological Science* 40, issue 2 (February, 2013), pp. 1279-1288.

Brown, Sarah K.; C.M. Darwent; E.J. Wictum; B.N. Sachs. 2015. "Using multiple markers to elucidate the ancient, historical and modern relationships among North American Arctic dog breeds." *Heredity*. 115, pp. 488-495.

Brunborg, Linn Anne; Kåre Julshamn; Ragnar Nortvedt; Livar Frøyland. "Nutritional Composition of Blubber and Meat of Hooded Seal (Cystophorura cristata) and Harp Seal (Phagophilus groenlandicus) from Greenland." *Food Chemistry*, Vol. 96, issue 4 (June, 2006), pp. 524-531.

Budiansky, Stephen. *The Truth about Dogs: The Ancestry, Social Conventions, Mental Habits and Moral Fibre of Canis familiaris*. Toronto, Ontario: Penguin Books Canada Ltd. 2000.

Cain, Johnny. "Hunting with Dogs." *Tumivut. (Oral Histories and firsthand stories of traditional life with Inuit Dogs)*. Published by Avataq Cultural Institute. Reprinted in *The Fan Hitch*. Vol. 14, No.1 (December, 2011).

Canadian Geographic. [VHS]. *Dog of the Midnight Sun. The Renaissance of the Canadian Inuit Husky*. Lillie, Ronald and Johnston, William (Executive Producers). La Rose, John (Producer/Director). Strange, Marc (Narrator). Produced by: Summerhill Entertainment. Inc. 2000.

Canadian Kennel Club website. www.ckc.ca.

Carpenter, William J. "Eskimo Dogs. All but forgotten and now near extinction." *Dogs in Canada*. (January, 1976).

"Taxonomy in Relation to the Inuit Dog and Major Historical References to the Breed." *The Fan Hitch*. Vol. 16, No. 2 (March, 2014),

Clutton-Brock, Juliet. *Eyewitness Books. DOG. Revised Edition*. New York, NY: DK Publishing, Inc. 2004.

Cohn, Jeffrey. "How Wild Wolves Became Domestic Dogs: Research Sheds New Light on the Origin of Humanity's Most Intimate Quadruple Ally." *Bio Science*. Vol 47, No. 11 (December, 1997).

Coppinger, Lorna with the International Sled Dog Racing Association. *The World of Sled Dogs. From Siberia to Sport Racing*. New York, NY: Howell Book House. 1977.

Coppinger, Raymond and Lorna. *Dogs. A Startling New Understanding of Canine Origin, Behaviour and Evolution*. New York, NY: Scribner. 2001.

Cox, Lynne. *South with the Sun. Roald Amundsen, his Polar explorations, & the Quest for Discovery*. New York, NY: Alfred A. Knopf. 2011.

Croteau, Jean-Jacques. *INTERIM REPORT. Allegations Concerning the Slaughter of Sled Dogs*. Submitted to the Makivik Corporation and the Government of Quebec. Anjou, QC. April 15, 2009.

Cummins, Bryan D. *First Nations, First Dogs*. Calgary, AB: Detselig Enterprises Ltd. 2002.

Cuvier, Jean Nicolas Léopold Frédéric (Georges Cuvier); Henry McMurtrie. *Cuvier's Animal Kingdom: Arranged according to its Organization*. Translated from the French and abridged for the use of students by McMurtie, H. London, Orr & Smith. 1834. Reprinted and published by HardPress Publishing. Miami, FL.

D'Allieso, Renate. "Bred to Survive: Canada's Iconic Sled Dogs face their greatest threat." *Globe and Mail*. (December 25, 2012).

Derr, Mark. *How the Dog Became the Dog: From Wolves to Our Best Friends*. London, New York: Overlook Duckworth. 2011.

Desmarest, M.A.G. *Mammalogie ou dèscription des èspèces de mammifères. Première Partie contenant les ordres des bimanes, des quadrumanes et des carnassiers*. Paris: Chez Mme Veuve Agasse, Imprimeur-libraire, 1820.

Ding, Z. L. et al. 2012. "Origins of Domestic Dog in Southern East Asia is Supported by Analysis of Y-chromosome DNA." *Heredity*: 108, pp. 507-514.

Dovers, Robert. *Huskies*. London: G. Bell and Sons. 1957.

Ehrlich, Gretel. *In the Empire of Ice: Encounters in a Changing Landscape*. Washington, DC: National Geographic. 2010.

Fédération Cynologique Internationale website. www.fci.be.

Flowers, Pam with Ann Dixon. *Alone across the Arctic: One Woman's Epic Journey by Dog Team*. Ortland, OR. Alaska Northwest Books. 2001.

Fox Gearheard, Shari. "Pangaggujjiniq Nunavut Quest 2015." *The Fan Hitch*. Vol. 17, No. 3 (June, 2015).

Fram Museum. Polar explorer Otto Sverdrup. Oslo, Norway. www.frammuseum.no.

Francis, Daniel. 2015. "Roald Amundsen." *Canadian Encyclopedia*.

Friis-Anderson, Hanne. "Greenland Dog / Canadian Inuit Dog ... it makes no difference." *The Fan Hitch*. Vol 7, No. 4. (September 2005).

Friis-Andersen, Hanne. Thesis. *Population Genetic Analysis of the Greenland Dog and Canadian Inuit Dog – Is it the Same Breed?* Royal Veterinary and Agricultural University, Department of Animal Science and Animal Health, Division of Animal Genetics. 2005.

Gallant, Johan & Edith. "Breed, Landrace and Purity: What do they mean?" In: *The Fan Hitch*. Vol 13, No. 1 (December, 2010).

Gearheard, Jake. "Qimmivut. Our Dogs." *The Fan Hitch*. Vol 13, No. 3 (June, 2011).

Gerstad, Ole and Joelie Sanguya. [DVD] *Qimmit. A Clash of Two Truths*. Produced by National Film Board of Canada and Piksuk Media. 2010.

Gerth, Nadine. "Living at the extremes – physiological adaptations of Inuit Sled Dogs in Greenland." *The Fan Hitch*. Vol. 9, No. 4 (September, 2007).

"Out on the Ice: Three days with Inuit Sled Dogs in North Greenland." *The Fan Hitch*. Vol. 10, No. 3 (June, 2008).

"Alternatives in physiological research using non-invasive methods in field biology." *The Fan Hitch*. Vol. 10, No. 4 (September 2008).

Gerth, Nadine; Redman, Paula; Speakman, John; Jackson, Sue; Starck, J. Matthias. 2010. "Energy metabolism of Inuit Sled Dogs." *Journal of Comparative Physiology B*. 180: 577-589.

Gordon, Allen. "Amaruit. Wolves Causing Havoc among Dog Owners in Kuujuaq." *The Fan Hitch*. Vol. 8, No. 1 (December, 2005).

Grimm, David. 2015. *Arctic Find Confirms Ancient Origin of Dogs*.

Hailor, Frank. Cardiff University. *Why Dog Breeds Aren't Considered Separate Species*.

Hamilton, Sue. "What is the ISDI?" *The Fan Hitch*. Vol. 6, No.1 (December, 2003).

"Featured Inuit Dog Owner Daniel Annanack." *The Fan Hitch*. Vol. 8, No.1 (December, 2005).

The Inuit Sled Dog. Article presented by the Primitive and Aboriginal Dog Society (PADS) at the first international conference "Aboriginal Breeds of Dogs as Elements of Biodiversity and Cultural Heritage of Humankind" held in Almaty, Kazakhstan in September 2007.

"Defining the Inuit Dog: Canis familiaris borealis." *The Fan Hitch*. Vol. 16, No. 2 (January, 2014).

Herbert, Wally. *Across the Top of the World: The British Trans-Arctic Expedition*. London: Longmans. 1969.

Heyes, Scott A. and Kristofer M. Helgen (editors). *Mammals of Ungava and Labrador. The 1882-1884 Field Notes of Lucien M. Turner together with Inuit and Innu Knowledge*. Published by Smithsonian Institution Scholarly Press, 2014.

Jenness, Diamond. *Through Darkening Spectacles*. Gatineau, QC: Museum of Civilization. 2008.

*Arctic Odyssey: The Diary of Diamond Jenness. 1913-1916*. Edited by Stuart E. Jenness. Gatineau, QC: Canadian Museum of Civilization. 1991.

Kaplan, Lawrence. 2011. *Inuit or Eskimo? Which name to use?* Alaska Native Language Center. University of Alaska, Fairbanks.

Knight, Charles (1791-1873). "Dogs Wild and Domestic." *Knight's Penny Magazine*. Vol. 10, p. 8. London: Charles Knight. 1832.

Kreeger, Terry J. "The Internal Wolf; Physiology, Pathology and Pharmacology." *Wolves* (David Mech, editor). Chicago: University of Chicago Press. 2003.

Leonard, Jennifer A.; Vilà, Carles; Wayne, Robert K. "From Wild Wolf to Domestic Dog." *The Dog and its Genome* (eds. Ostrander, Elaine A., Giger, Urs, Lindblad-Toh, Kerstin). pp. 95-112. New York, NY: Cold Spring Harbor Laboratory Press. 2006.

Lévesque, Francis. "Investigating the Inuit-Canadian Government Relationship. Claiming about the Fate of Inuit Dogs and Inuit leadership." *Études Inuit*. Val d'Or: October 2010.

Lyon, Captain G.F. *Private Journal of Captain G.F. Lyon of H.M.S. Hecla During the Recent Voyage of Discovery under Captain Parry.* London: John Murray, Albemarle-street. 1824.

MacRury, Ian Kenneth. 1991. [Master's Thesis]. *The Inuit Dog: Its Provenance, Environment and History.* Scott Polar Research Institute. University of Cambridge. Cambridge, UK. (4th printing, Sept. 2006).

Makivik Corporation. SUBMISSION to the Minister of Indian and Northern Affairs for the Government of Canada and To the Ministre délégué aux Affaires autochtones for the Government of Québec. Regarding the Slaughtering of Nunavik "Qimmiit" (Inuit Dogs) from the mid-1950s to the late 1960s. January, 2005.

Malauri, Jean. *The Last Kings of Thule: With the Polar Eskimoes as They Face their Destiny.* University of Chicago Press. 1985.

Martin, W.C.L. (1798-1864). *The History of the Dog: Its Origin, Physical and Moral Characteristics, and its Principal Varieties.* London: Charles Knight & Co.

McHugh, Susan. University of New England. 2013. "A Flashpoint in Inuit Memories: Endangered Knowledge in the Mountie Sled Dog Massacre." *ESC (English Studies in Canada)* 39.1 (March), pp. 149-175.

Mech, L. David & Luigi Boitani (editors). *WOLVES: Behavior, Ecology, Conservation.* Chicago, Ill: University of Chicago Press. 2003.

Mikkelse, Peter Schmidt. "About the Sirius Patrol." *The Fan Hitch.* Vol. 7, No. 1 (December, 2004).

Miles Kim and Haynes, Jody. 2008. "From Wolf to Dog: Genetics and Domestication." *Florida Lupine News.* Vol. 10 (3).

Milius, S. "Three Dog Eves: Canine diaspora from East Asia to Americas." *Science News*, November 20, 2002.

Montcombroux, (2nd edition). *The Canadian Inuit Dog: Canada's Heritage.* Inwood, MB: Whipoorwill Press. 2002.

"The Inuit Sled Dog International's Official Stand on the Issue of Blue Eyes in Inuit Sled Dogs." *The Fan Hitch.* Vol. 5, No. 1 (December. 2002).

Morey, Darcy F. and Kim Aaris-Sørensen. "Paleoeskimo dogs of the Eastern Arctic." 2002. *Arctic.* 55, No. 1, pp. 44-56. Arctic Institute of North America of the University of Calgary.

Morrison, David and Georges-Hébert Germain. *Inuit Glimpses of an Arctic Past.* Hull, QC: Canadian Museum of Civilization. 1995.

National Human Genome Research Institute. National Institute of Health. *Talking Glossary of Genetic Terms.*

National Park Service. *Bering Land Bridge. History and Culture.*

Nickerson, Sheila. *Harnessed to the Pole. Sledge Dogs in Service to American Explorers of the Arctic, 1853-1909.* Fairbanks. University of Alaska Press. 2014.

Nowak, Ronald M. "Wolf Evolution and Taxonomy." *WOLVES: Behavior, Ecology, Conservation.* (Editors: Mech, David L., Luigi Boitani). Chicago: University of Chicago Press: 2003.

Nunavut Quest website. www.nunavutquest.com.

Nygaard, Ove. "Blue Eyes in Norway's Greenland Dogs." *The Fan Hitch.* Vol. 5, No. 1 (December, 2002).

Ostrander, Elaine and Robert K. Wayne. "The Canine Genome." *Genome Research.* Cold Spring Laboratory Press. 2005.

Park, Robert W. The Arctic Institute of North America. *Dog Remains from Devon Island, NWT. Archaeological and Osteological Evidence for Domestic Dog Use in the Thule Culture.* Department of Anthropology. University of Alberta. Calgary, AB. 1987.

Pastore, Ralph T. 1998. Newfoundland and Labrador Heritage website. www.heritage.nf.ca.

PBS. Nature. 2010. *Dogs That Changed the World.* Interview: Molecular Biologist Peter Savolainen. Educational Broadcasting Corporation.

PBS. Nature. *Dogs that Changed the World. What caused the Domestication of Wolves?*

Peplinski, Lynn. 1996. "The Dogs of the Inuit: Companions in Survival." *World Animal Review.* 86.

Polarworld. "Sir Wally Herbert: Icon of Polar Exploration." www.polarworld.co.uk.

Qikiqtani Inuit Association. 2013. Qikiqtani Truth Commission. Thematic Reports and Special Studies. 1950-1975. Qimmiliriniq: Inuit Sled Dogs in Qikiqtaaluk.

2013. Qikiqtani Truth Commission. Thematic Reports and Special Studies. 1950-1975. QTC Final Report: Achieving Saimaqatiqiingniq.

Rennie, James. *Natural History of Quadrupeds.* New York. Harper & Bros. 1840.

Roach, John. 2009. "Dogs First Tamed in China — to be Food?" *National Geographic News.* September 4.

Ross, John F. 2004. "Top Dogs." *Smithsonian Magazine.* (January).

Royal Canadian Mounted Police. 2006. Final Report: RCMP Review of Allegations Concerning Inuit Sled Dogs.

Rutherford, Clarice. *A Dog is a Dog: And that's why he's so special.* Crawford, CO: Alpine Publications. 2013.

Ryne, Linn. "Where none have gone before: The Life of Roald Amundsen." *Great Norwegians.*

Saey, Tina Hesman. 2015. "Ancient DNA Pushes Back Timing of Origin of Dogs: Ancestors of domesticated canines may have split from wolves as early as 40,000 years ago." *Science News.* June 13, 2015.

2017. "Dog domestication happened just once, ancient DNA study suggests." *Science News.* July 18.

Sanna, Ellyn & Hunter, William. *Canada's Modern-Day First Nations. Nunavut and Evolving Relationships.* Philadelphia, PA: Mason Crest Publishers. 2006.

Savolainen, Peter; Ya-ping Zhang, Jing Luo, Joakim Lundeberg, and Thomas Leitner (2002-11-22). "Genetic Evidence for an East Asian Origin of Domestic Dogs." *Science* 298 (5598): pp. 1610–1613.

Savolainen, Peter. "Wiege der Hunde. Studie über den Ursprung der Hunde." (Cradle of Dogs. A Study into the Origin of Dogs). *Hundemagazin WUFF.* 2014. Vol. 3/04 pp. 38-41 and Vol. 4/04, pp. 42-46.

"mtDNA Studies of the Origin of Dogs." *The Dog and its Genome.* New York: Cold Spring Harbor Laboratory Press. 2006.

"Investigation of the pre-Columbian Ancestry of Today's Dogs of the Americas." *The Fan Hitch.* Vol. 16, No.1 (December, 2013).

Savolainen, Peter; Zhang, Ya-Ping; Luo, Jing; Lundeberg, Joakim; Leitner, Thomas. "Genetic evidence for an East Asian Origin of Domestic Dogs." *Science* 298 (5598): 1610-1613. 2002.

Schleidt, Wolfgang/Michael D. Shalter. 2003. "Co-Evolution of Humans and Canids. An Alternative View of Dog Domestication: Homo Homini Lupus?" *Evolution and Cognition.* Vol. 9, No. 1, pp. 57-72.

Schwartz, Marion. *A History of Dogs in the Early Americas.* New Haven, London: Yale University Press. 1997.

Secretariat of the Antarctic Treaty. 2016. Non-native Species Manual.

Secretariat of the Antarctic Treaty. 2016. Annex II to the Protocol on Environmental Protection to the Antarctic Treaty. Conservation of Antarctic Fauna and Flora.

Shannon, Kerrie Ann. [Master's thesis] *The Unique Role of Sled dogs in Inuit Culture: An examination of the Relationship between Inuit Sled Dogs in the Changing North.* University of Alberta. Department of Anthropology. 1997.

"An Examination of Traditional Knowledge: The Case of the Inuit Sled Dog." Part 3/4. *The Fan Hitch.* Vol. 12, No. 3 (June, 2010).

Skafte, Peter. "Knud Rasmussen. Arctic explorer and anthropologist." www.arcticthule.com.

Skoglund, Pontus; Ersmark, Erik; Palkopoulou, Eleftheria; Dalén, Love. "Ancient Wolf Genome Shows an early divergence of Domestic Dog Ancestors and Admixture into High Latitude Breeds." *Current Biology*, Vol. 25, issue 11, pp. 1515-1519. Published online May 21, 2015.

Smith, Charles Hamilton (1776-1859). "Dogs." Volume 2. *The Naturalist's Library*. (Edited by Sir William Jardine, Bart). London: Henry G. Bohn. 1839.

Trut, Lyudmilla. 1999. "Early Canid Domestication. The Farm Fox Experiment." *American Scientist*. Vol. 87 (2), pp.160-169.

University of Calgary. Applied History Research Group. *Canada's First Nations*.

Tiffany-Castiglioni, Evelyn. 2001. "The Domestication of the Dog." Part I. *Forum on Science and Technology. Phi Kappa Phi Forum*. Vol. 84, No. 3.

2004. "The Domestication of the Dog." Part II. *Forum on Science and Technology. Phi Kappa Phi Forum*. Vol. 85, No. 1.

Vila, Carles; Savolainen, Peter; Maldonado, Jesus E.; Amorim, Isabel R.; Rice, John E.; Honeycutt, Rodney L.; Crandall, Keith A.; Lundeberg, Joakim; Wayne, Robert (1997-01-30; accepted 1997-04-14). "Multiple and Ancient Origins of the Domestic Dog." *Science* 276: 1687–1689.

Wade, Nicholas. "New Findings Puts Origin of Dogs in Middle East." *The New York Times*. March 17, 2010.

Walker, John. *Arctic Defenders. A Story of Visionary Inuit with a Dream: The Creation of Nunavut*. DVD.

Walker, Richard. *Genes and DNA*. Boston, Mass.: Kingfisher. 2003.

Wang, Xiaoming and Tedford, Richard H. *DOGS. Their Fossil Relatives and Evolutionary History*. New York: Columbia University Press. 2008.

Watt-Cloutier, Sheila. *The Right to be Cold*. Toronto: Allen Lane. 2015.

Wayne, Robert K. and Carles Vila. "Molecular Genetic Studies of Wolves." *Wolves: Behavior, Ecology, and Conservation*. (Editors: Mech, L. David, Boitani, Luigi), pp. 218-238. Chicago: University of Chicago Press. 2003.

Wayne, Robert et al. 2010. "Genome-wide SNP and Haplotype Analyses Reveal a Rich History of Underlying Dog Domestication." *Nature* (April).

Whitcomb, Ed. *A Short History of the Canadian North*. Ottawa, ON: From Sea to Sea Enterprises. 2010.

Whitelaw, Ian. *Snow Dogs! Racers of the North*. Toronto: DK Publishing. 2008.

Willmer, Pat, Stone, Graham, Johnston, Ian. "Extreme Terrestrial Habitats." *Environmental Physiology of Animals*. 2nd edition, pp. 210-211 and 658-9. Oxford: Blackwell Publishing, United Kingdom. 2005.

Wolpert, Stuart. 2013. UCLA Newsroom. Dogs likely originated in Europe more than 18,000 years ago, UCLA biologists report (November 14).

Siu-Ling riding into
the sunset with
her beloved dogs.
*Photo: Thomas
Godfrey.*

# MORE BOOKS BY REVODANA PUBLISHING

Little Kids and Their Big Dogs:  Volumes 1, 2 and 3

The Leonberger:  A Comprehensive Guide to the Lion King of Breeds

Everyone's Guide to the Bullmastiff

The Official Book of the Neapolitan Mastiff

The Afghan Hound: Interviews with the Breed Pioneers

The Best of Babbie:  The Wicked Wisdom of Babbie Tongren,
the Afghan Hound's Sharpest Wit

Your Rhodesian Ridgeback Puppy:  The Ultimate Guide to
Finding, Rearing and Appreciating the Best Companion Dog in the World

Exploring the Tibetan Mastiff: A Love Letter in Photographs

# ESPECIALLY FOR CHILDREN

Peyton Goes to the Dog Show

How the Rhodesian Ridgeback Got Its Ridge

Visit www.revodanapublishing.com

CPSIA information can be obtained
at www.ICGtesting.com
Printed in the USA
LVHW072058010519
616326LV00001B/6/P